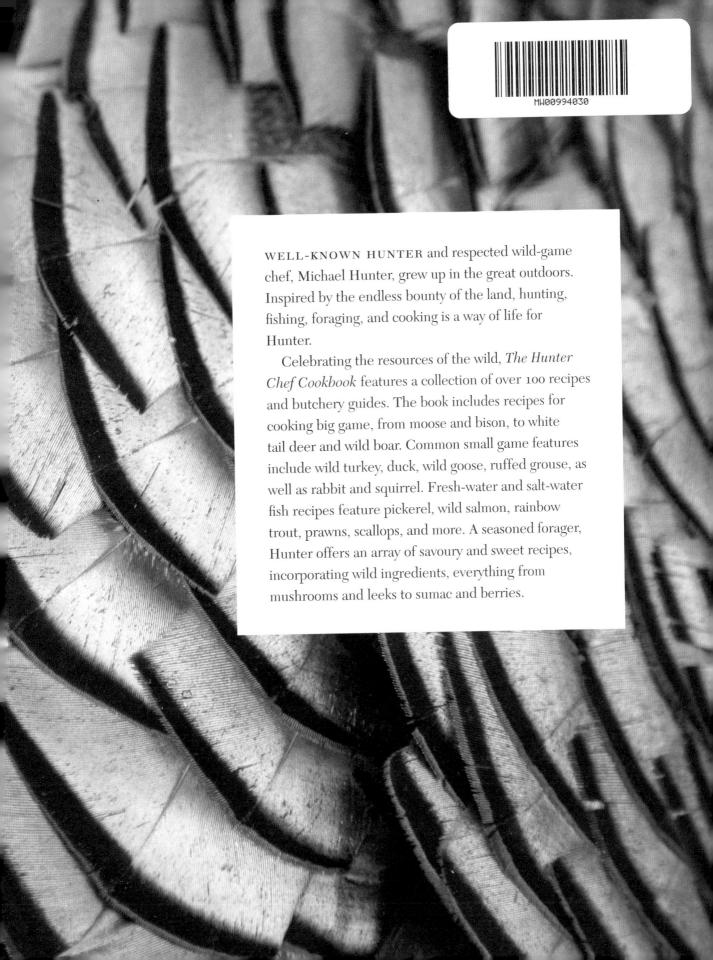

WELL-KNOWN HUNTER and respected wild-game chef, Michael Hunter, grew up in the great outdoors. Inspired by the endless bounty of the land, hunting, fishing, foraging, and cooking is a way of life for Hunter.

Celebrating the resources of the wild, *The Hunter Chef Cookbook* features a collection of over 100 recipes and butchery guides. The book includes recipes for cooking big game, from moose and bison, to white tail deer and wild boar. Common small game features include wild turkey, duck, wild goose, ruffed grouse, as well as rabbit and squirrel. Fresh-water and salt-water fish recipes feature pickerel, wild salmon, rainbow trout, prawns, scallops, and more. A seasoned forager, Hunter offers an array of savoury and sweet recipes, incorporating wild ingredients, everything from mushrooms and leeks to sumac and berries.

THE HUNTER CHEF
COOKBOOK

Hunt, Fish, and Forage in
Over 100 Recipes

Michael Hunter

Photography by Jody Shapiro
and Michael Hunter

PENGUIN

an imprint of Penguin Canada, a division of Penguin Random House Canada Limited

Canada • USA • UK • Ireland • Australia • New Zealand • India • South Africa • China

First published 2020

www.penguinrandomhouse.ca

Library and Archives Canada Cataloguing in Publication

Title: The hunter chef cookbook: hunt, fish, and forage in over 100 recipes / Michael Hunter.
Names: Hunter, Michael (Chef), author.
Identifiers: Canadiana (print) 20200172972 | Canadiana (ebook) 20200172980 | ISBN 9780735236943 (hardcover) |
    ISBN 9780735236950 (HTML)
Subjects: LCSH: Cooking (Game) | LCSH: Cooking (Fish) | LCSH: Cooking (Wild foods) | LCGFT: Cookbooks.
Classification: LCC TX751 .H86 2020 | DDC 641.6/9—dc23

Cover and interior design by Leah Springate
Photography, food, and prop styling by Jody Shapiro and Michael Hunter
Cover photography by Jody Shapiro
Photo on pages 7 and 66 by Del Mahabadi
Printed and bound in China

10 9 8 7 6 5 4 3 2

Penguin
Random House
PENGUIN CANADA

To my children—you are my daily inspiration to succeed in life.
Without you, I would be lost.
Let this book show you anything is possible
as long as you put your mind to it.

CONTENTS

LARGE GAME

SMALL GAME

FISH AND FORAGE

WILD DESSERTS AND FORAGED COCKTAILS

INTRODUCTION

I AM A HUNTER BY NAME and by nature. And I'm a chef by training. It's only natural that those two worlds would come together. Food is more than a passion for me; it is a way of life. Hunting, fishing, foraging, and cooking fulfill a primal urge. I am a true hunter-gatherer at heart. Sometimes I feel like I was born a few hundred years too late.

As a professional chef for most of my life, I have always taken pride in being able to hunt what I cook. It seems to me that people have forgotten where their food comes from. Food that is locally sourced or raised in its natural environment is healthier and more nutritious than something that's been living in a cramped pen for months or is flown halfway around the world before it gets to your table. In contrast, walking into the forest with your family and returning with nourishments that you sourced together and then prepare for your dinner is a beautiful learning experience. Allowing others to live that experience is exactly what I want this book to be about.

My cooking career began when I was thirteen. I rode my bike to the local gas station and applied for a position to pump gas. Fortunately for me, the employer only had a position in the kitchen of the diner he owned across the parking lot. I started out on the breakfast shift, making toast and hash browns and washing dishes for a few months before graduating to flipping eggs and working the flat-top griddle. I was in high school and getting up at six on weekends to bike thirty minutes to work at a diner that had lineups out the door. And that's when I discovered my drive to succeed; I loved to eat and I loved to cook, and that proved to be a real motivation.

A few years later I applied to work at the local golf course after hearing from my friends that it paid better and there were cute girls who also worked there. Again working the breakfast shift, I was quickly noticed for my speed and talent, and I began to stick around to help out in the evenings and work banquets and weddings. It was quite a change for me, cooking steaks and roasts of prime rib and giant vats of mashed potatoes, and assembling hundreds of plates at a time. When I worked nights I also became chummy with the bartenders, who would slip us kitchen guys drinks in exchange for food. As an underage punk kid, I thought this was a great trade.

In the off-season from the golf course I earned my keep at the Belfountain Inn, a small country inn in the village of Belfountain, Ontario. It was a cozy and quaint thirty-six-seat dining room in an old Victorian home on the Credit River. That restaurant proved to be the game-changer in my career. It is where my true passion for cooking was born.

At the golf club, mashed potatoes came from a frozen bag and the jus was from packaged powder. But at the Belfountain Inn everything was made from scratch. I learned how to make fresh pasta, sauces, vinaigrettes, desserts, and even organic tofu. Here was where I discovered the art of a true chef life. I was hooked.

Soon after beginning my work at the inn, I learned at 18 years old I was going to become a father. I had to make an important decision on how I was going to support my new family and choose cooking as a career. I enrolled in culinary college and began my formal training to become a chef. School brought me back to the basics in a structured environment, and although I had been in kitchens from a young age, it helped me continue to hone my skills.

But my real education, the path that helped me transition from Chef Michael Hunter to the Hunter Chef, was when I was working with Graham Black and Dave McRae at the Old Cataract Inn, where they taught me about foraging. We would forage for mushrooms, watercress, mint, and other herbs across the street in the valley and feature them in the restaurant that night. My eyes were opened to how special these ingredients were because of their flavour and freshness.

My quest for pure ingredients then led to hunting. I wanted to eat food that was untainted by hormones and pesticides and to learn as much as I could about natural food and organic farming. This was the period of my life that cemented who I am today. I discovered that hunting and foraging, and being inspired by the resources of the land, could lead to profound creativity in a professional kitchen.

Unfortunately, at that time, putting wild foods on the menu wasn't always the easiest sell conceptually. It was 2013. I was the executive chef at an upscale Toronto restaurant. I had achieved everything I had aimed for, but I was bored and frustrated. I wanted to cook the food I wanted to serve to people, but my bosses kept saying *wait*. I wanted to introduce game dishes, but they were always turning me down.

Then I met my business partner, Jody Shapiro, a Toronto filmmaker and photographer with a strong interest in cooking. We came to an agreement: Jody would take photographs for a book that I wanted to put out about hunting and cooking. In exchange, I would teach Jody how to cook.

The more pictures Jody took in the field, the more he became interested in hunting and foraging and in the link between the wild and the plate. And I witnessed first-hand that the more you could educate people about where their food comes from, the more interest they would have about consciously sourcing their ingredients. It was everything I had hoped would happen by sharing my knowledge of where our food comes from.

Jody and I started to explore the potential for a game-focused restaurant. We started doing game dinners, private events devoted to the rich variety of local game and foraged foods, all of it hunted and collected by me. We developed a following on social media, and with so much interest, we knew it was time to make a permanent home—a place where we could work on this book, and where I could cook what I wanted to cook. For two guys without much business experience, against all odds, we opened our own restaurant.

Deer is one of my favourite game animals. I love hunting them, and venison is one of my favourite dishes. What's left after you've used every part of the deer? The antlers. It is no coincidence that shed antlers are treasured finds for foragers—who else is scouring the forest floor on the lookout for wild leeks and morels? So the restaurant named itself: Antler. The name symbolizes hunting, meat, the outdoors, nature, foraging—everything I'm about and everything I celebrate. It's more than a brand. It's a lifestyle.

In our first few months, we had a chicken entrée in case there were diners who wanted to play it safe. It was a great dish, but we were only selling two a night. We ate them for staff meals. It just wasn't worth keeping on the menu—which was a good sign. The notion of trying new things is baked into the DNA of Antler. People come expecting something different, and we give it to them. Ultimately your guests determine what will stay on the menu. You can put anything you like on a menu, but if people don't order it, there's nothing you can do.

Antler has now been going for five years, and I'm still serving dishes that excite me. We have deer, wild boar, pheasant, duck, bison, and wild fish on our menu. Our staff goes on regular foraging trips as a team, preparing what we find for diners. New patrons keep arriving and regulars keep coming back.

And so, in keeping with the Antler spirit and the journey I've taken to get to this point in my career, this cookbook centres on my love of using wild ingredients—edible plants, game animals, wild fish and seafood—to create contemporary dishes that can be served both at the restaurant and at home. Every recipe contains at least one ingredient that is hunted, fished, or foraged (with suggestions for grocery-store substitutions, of course). In this book you can follow me both into the woods and back to the kitchen, to learn how to live off the land from the "fruits of the forest."

Although certain parts of this book may appeal to professionals in the kitchen, I have written it for home cooks looking to expand their skills and repertoire by teaching about the regional ingredients that can be found throughout North America.

The Canadian culinary experience can be hard to define—we have so many rich cultures, such a long history, and the country is so vast, with varying flora and fauna, that no one dish can characterize us. But the bounty of what this land provides is endless. And there is no reason why we can't celebrate the use of wild ingredients that sometimes we can find right in our backyard. Whether morel mushrooms on a damp spring morning, or wild ginger during a hike with your kids, or the deer you've been patiently waiting in a tree stand for hours hoping to spot—once you know what you're seeking out in the wild, you'll eventually see it.

Cooking with ingredients found in the wilderness can take you on some wonderful journeys. I hope this book encourages you to join in the adventure, both in and outside of the kitchen.

BUTCHERY GUIDES

HOW TO BUTCHER A DEER

BUTCHERING YOUR OWN DEER IS incredibly satisfying. It will give you a better understanding of the animal and how to cook the various cuts. You will see the tendons, the silverskin, and fat. You feel the softer texture of the tenderloins and backstraps and the firmness of the legs, shoulder cuts, and neck meat.

Butchering your own game also saves you a lot of money you'd otherwise pay someone else to process your meat. You do not need a lot of fancy tools and gadgets. An entire deer can be processed with nothing more than a sharp 5- to 7-inch (12 to 18 cm) boning knife. However, a cleaver and hacksaw can come in handy for making fancier cuts like frenching the racks (trimming and exposing the bones along the ribs). If you plan to process a lot of large animals, a reciprocating saw is a great investment that will save you time; a good one costs under a hundred dollars.

Once the deer has been gutted and skinned, I like to hang the meat for at least twenty-four to forty-eight hours, to allow the rigor mortis to relax and to air-dry the meat slightly. Depending on the time of year, deer are usually quite lean, and hanging for too long can excessively dry out the meat. Generally, hanging a skinned deer for three to five days is perfect. If you have a cooler, dry-aging with the skin on can help retain the tenderness of the meat, but it makes it more challenging to remove the hide.

The next thing I do is break down the whole deer into six parts. In the picture on the right, I have cut the deer into eight pieces—the head, neck, rib cage, two front legs, torso, and two back legs.

1. Start by removing the head. With a boning knife, cut along the back of the skull. Find the joint where the spine meets the skull and cut 360 degrees around the spine. Cut into the connective tissue between the joints of the spine, then twist the skull to snap it off.

2. Remove the neck where it meets the front of the shoulders and rib cage. Cut 360 degrees around the base of the neck where it meets the top of the shoulders. You will cut through several inches of meat at the base of the neck before you reach the spine. Cut into the connective tissue between the joints of the spine and twist to snap and remove the neck.

3. Remove the front legs by pulling them away from the chest and cutting through the connective tissue under the shoulders. There is no ball joint connecting the front leg to the body, just connective tissue.

4. To remove the rib cage, find the last bone on the rib cage. Cut behind the last rib bone, cutting down until the knife hits the spine. Repeat on the other side. Cut through the meat (loins/backstraps) on each side of the spine, then pull the rib cage back to snap the spine and remove the rib cage.

5. Finally, remove the back legs from the hip. Working on one side first, and starting from the inside of the spine, locate the hip. Cut around the inside of the hip, then push the leg out and away from the hip. Cutting down and pulling the leg back, the ball joint should now be visible. Cut around the ball joint. Cut towards the back of the hip, doing your best to hug the bone with the tip of your knife, and cut off the back leg. Repeat on the other side.

Breaking Down the Back Legs

The back leg of a deer has a few muscles that can be cut into steaks or roasted whole, such as the inside round, outside round, and eye of round. The rest of the meat can be cut into stewing chunks or ground in a meat grinder. Using a thin boning knife and your fingers, you can easily pull apart and separate these muscle groups. Start by making a very shallow cut following the white sinew lines and gently pulling with your fingers.

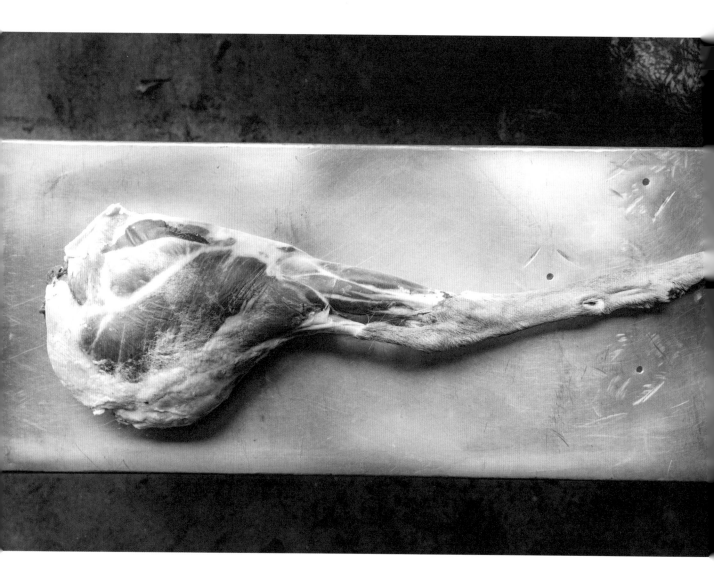

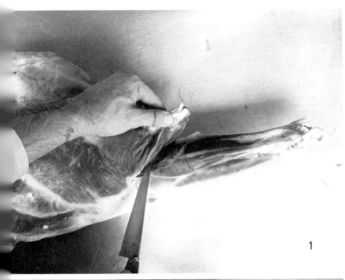

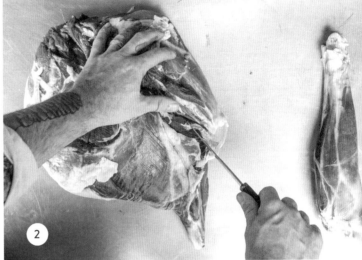

1. Remove the hoof by cutting 360 degrees around the joint. Cut the sinew and connective tissue around the joint. Apply pressure with your hands to snap the joint. Cut along the shank following the sinew line.

2. Cut along the inside sinew lines on the inside of the leg to expose the femur bone.

3. Cut around the femur bone lengthwise, hugging the bone on all sides to remove it.

4. Separate the muscle groups by cutting along the sinew lines.

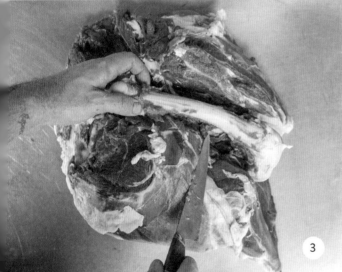

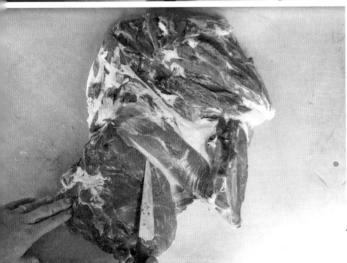

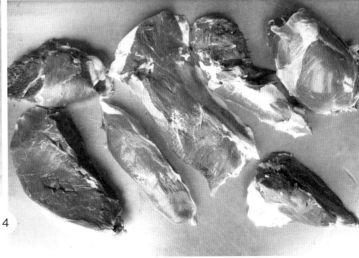

Deer Cuts

Following are the separated muscle groups that can be roasted whole or cut horizontally for steaks.

Two striploins (backstraps) and two tenderloins To remove the striploins and tenderloins from the spine, make an L-shaped cut down, hugging the spine and out along the vertebrae. These cuts are perfect for grilling steaks. I recommend not cooking past medium doneness for these cuts.

Frenched rack To remove the racks with the rib bones attached, working from the outside of the rib cage, use a thin boning knife to make a long cut downward along the entire spine, separating the loin from the spine. To cut the bones underneath, you can use a sharp cleaver, wire cutters, a hacksaw or a reciprocating saw. Cut the rib bones where they meet the spine from the bottom/inside the rib cavity. The term frenched means to clean the bones above the loin creating a cleaned bone chop.

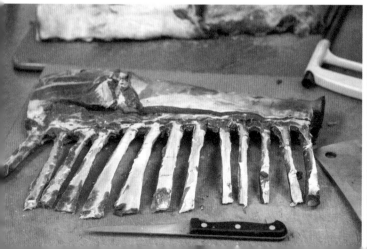 

Neck pot roast Cut the neck into 3- to 4-inch (8 to 10 cm) sections by cutting 360 degrees around the spine, then cutting through the bone with a cleaver or hacksaw.

Shoulder, arm, and shank 1 whole front leg, left to right, shoulder blade, arm, forearm/shank. These cuts are best for stewing or grinding.

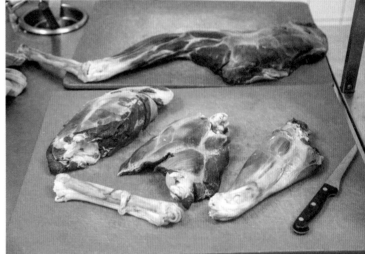

Offal Deer offal should be eaten fresh within a few days of harvesting or frozen as soon as possible. Heart and liver shown here.

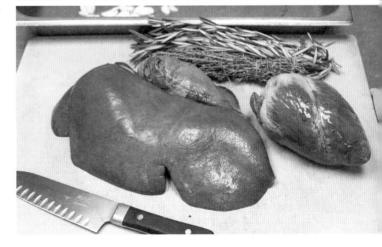

HOW TO BUTCHER A DUCK

WATERFOWL HUNTING IS MOSTLY DONE with nontoxic pellets. Shots are aimed at the head, but sometimes a few pellets find their way into the breast and leg meat. If lead is legal to use, you must be very careful to remove all pellets and meat that has come in contact with lead. Even if using nontoxic lead, it is important to remove the pellets and damaged meat, as contamination from bacteria is possible.

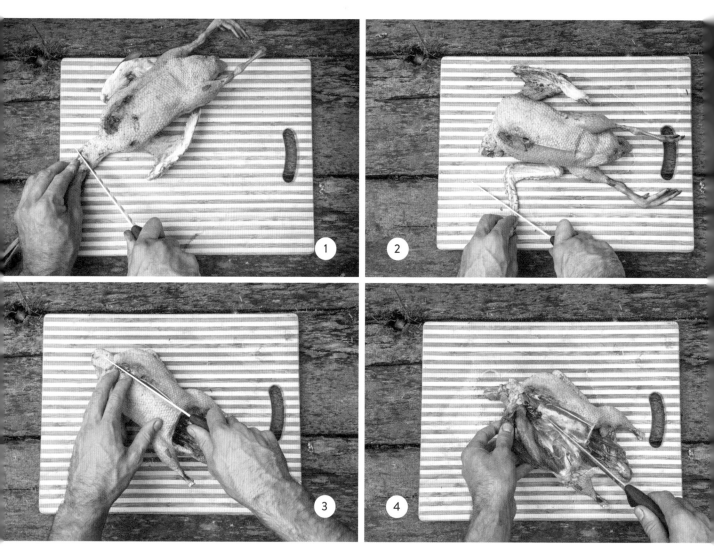

1. Remove the neck: Using a sharp boning knife or chef's knife, cut through the base of neck where the neck meets the top of the breast meat.

2. Cut and trim the wing tips: Remove the wings. Cut through the middle of the joint just below the wing tip. Then cut the joint between the wing and drumette.

3. Position the bird with the breasts up. Make a cut beside the breastbone. Feel the middle of the breast meat to find the breastbone that runs down the centre. Hugging the bone with the blade, make a cut down the length of the breast meat on one side.

4. Continue to slice along the ribs, hugging the blade along the bones. Pull the breast meat back and cut under the meat, hugging the rib bones, to remove the breast meat from the body with the drumette attached to the breast.

5. Slice around the cavity with your knife to the back of the carcass, slicing down towards the tail to remove the leg and breast in one piece.

6. Cut along the inside of the thigh and drumstick bones so the meat will lie flat in a skillet. Cut away any tendon and sinew.

7. Repeat steps 3 through 6 on the other side of the duck. If you have a kitchen torch, burn off any small feathers, or remove the small pin feathers with tweezers or needle-nose pliers.

HOW TO BUTCHER A WILD TURKEY

BUTCHERING A WILD TURKEY IS the same as butchering a chicken or duck, except it is a little larger. You can practise on chickens using the same method. Plucking the whole bird and cooking with the skin on is more flavourful and protects the meat from drying out. There is lots of meat on the legs, and with a little extra care these can provide a few valuable meals.

1. Pluck and gut the turkey: After shooting your bird, start plucking the feathers from the breast area. The feathers will come out much easier while the bird is still warm. Pull up on the skin below the breasts and make a shallow incision across the entire stomach, cutting upwards and being careful not to cut the intestines. Using your hand, pull out all the innards. Keep the heart, liver, and gizzard and discard the rest.

2. Remove the bottom leg just below the drumstick. Using a boning knife, cut 360 degrees around the knee joint. Cut the sinew and, using your hands, snap the joint in half.

3. Position the bird with the breasts up. Feel the middle of the breast meat to find the breastbone that runs down the centre. Hugging the bone with the blade, make a cut down the length of the breast meat on one side.

4. Continue to slice along the ribs, hugging the blade along the bones. Pull the breast meat back and cut under the meat, hugging the rib bones, to remove the breast meat from the body. Remove the legs by pulling the thigh away from the body and cutting down along the cavity of the bird. Simply pull back on the ball joint to pop it out. Continue cutting away the meat along the back of the bird to remove the leg.

5. Repeat steps 2 through 4 on the other side of the turkey.

6. Cut the legs from the breasts. Cut the skin holding the legs and breast together.

7. Separated breast and leg shown.

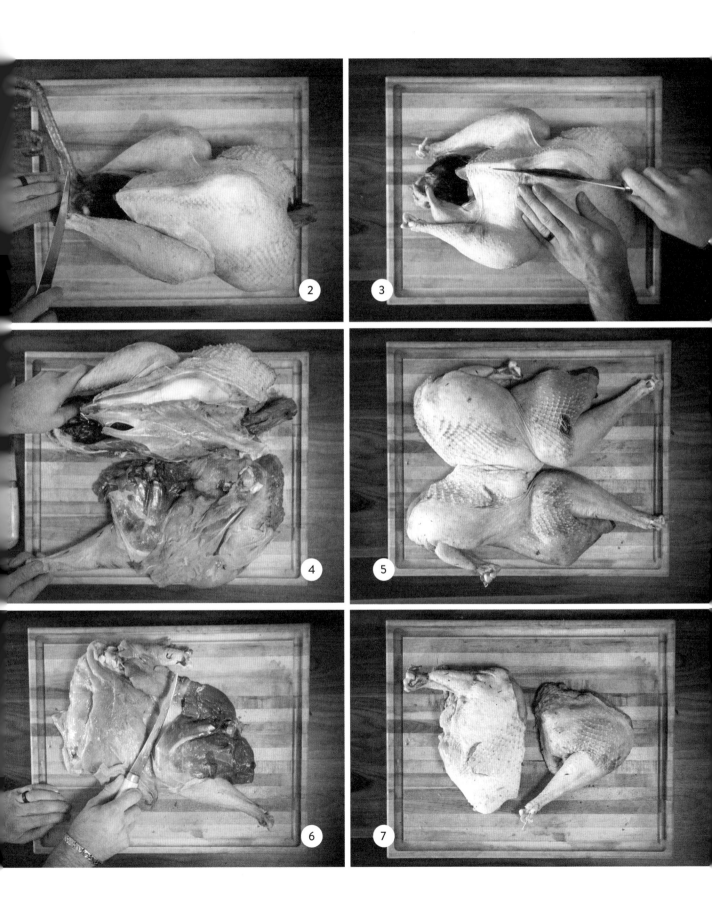

LARGE GAME

MY FOOD PHILOSOPHY

SOME OF MY MOST CONTEMPLATIVE moments are spent up in a tree, in my tree stand, waiting for a deer. That's when I get some of my best ideas for dishes, especially venison. When I'm up in a tree, I get more than a different perspective: I get philosophical.

There is no getting around the fact that if I am going to eat meat, an animal must die. Yet people will openly admit they do not want to know how that beautiful steak found its way behind the glass at their local butcher. They do not really want to know what they are eating. I have been to slaughterhouses, so I have seen it. I am much more comfortable eating something I killed myself, knowing that it lived a natural life in the wild. A deer in the wild *does not* die of old age. More likely, it starves to death or is devoured alive by coyotes or wolves.

My approach is to respect the animal by using every part I can. When I kill a deer, all of its meat from head to tail, including the liver, the kidneys, and the heart, goes into my freezer and onto my family's plates. I've used deer leather for a knife bag and an apron. My wedding ring was carved out of deer antler.

Animals in the wild eat a diverse range of food and are generally healthier than animals raised on factory farms and pumped full of hormones. Obviously, hunting is not for everyone, nor is it a practical solution for feeding millions. However, if you are going to eat meat, you should eat the best you can afford. Get to know your butcher. Ask where he or she sources the meat behind the glass.

Do not stop at meat. Go to farmers' markets, pull over on those country highways and buy fruits and vegetables straight from the field, or freshly laid eggs. Why buy strawberries in the winter that have been gassed so they ripen on the long ride up from California? We have Canadian pears and apples all winter long. Local tastes better and is better for you.

My food philosophy is simple: if you are what you eat, you should know what you are eating.

Grinding your own meat is a great way to use the whole animal. Every scrap or trimming I get from the animal goes through the grinder and gets used in sauces, stuffings, terrines, or, as here, burgers. The venison and bison are very similar in appearance and taste, while the wild boar adds both balance to the gamey flavour and fat to the mix. Cooking the burgers in a cast-iron pan will give the patties a caramelized flavour and crispy golden crust. You can grill the burgers over charcoal for smokier flavour.

GAME BURGER

Makes 8 burgers

In the bowl of a stand mixer fitted with the paddle attachment, or in a large bowl by hand, mix together the venison, wild boar, and bison. Divide the mixture into eight 6-ounce (170 g) portions and, using your hands or a burger patty press, shape into patties. Place the burgers on a baking sheet lined with parchment paper and store in the fridge, covered, for at least an hour. Chilling the burgers before searing will keep them from breaking apart.

Heat a large cast-iron skillet over high heat for 2 to 3 minutes.

Season both sides of the patties with a pinch each of salt and pepper. Add the grapeseed oil to the pan. Place the patties in the pan (working in batches if needed) and cook, flipping once or twice, for 2 to 3 minutes per side for medium-rare doneness. (Flipping too often can cause the burgers to fall apart and not get the desired flavourful crust on the outside.) Cook to an internal temperature of 125°F (50°C) for medium-rare doneness or 135°F (57°C) for medium doneness (pink).

Place each burger on the bottom of a toasted bun. Top with smoked cheddar cheese and your desired toppings. Top with the other bun half.

1 pound (450 g) ground venison
1 pound (450 g) ground wild boar
1 pound (450 g) ground bison
2 teaspoons (10 mL) kosher salt
1 teaspoon (5 mL) black pepper
2 tablespoons (30 mL) grapeseed oil or vegetable oil, for searing
8 hamburger buns, toasted

SUGGESTED TOPPINGS

8 slices smoked cheddar cheese
Sliced red onion
Sliced dill pickles
Sliced tomatoes
Garlic Aioli (page 38)
Hot mustard

This recipe is a great one for learning how to cure and dry-age charcuterie. The venison loin is a smaller piece of meat and does not take very long to cure and age compared with a leg of prosciutto, which hangs for about a year to dry-cure. This earthy, rich venison bresaola is delicious thinly sliced in a sandwich or on a pizza or charcuterie board.

When making your own dry-cured charcuterie at home, it is a good idea to buy a hygrometer to measure the humidity. Hygrometers are available in hardware stores. You will find curing salt (sodium nitrate) at your local butcher shop or online. I use Prague Powder #1.

VENISON BRESAOLA

Makes about 750 g dry-cured meat

Place the venison in a large thick resealable plastic bag or vacuum bag. Add the maple syrup, kosher salt, curing salt, juniper, thyme, and rosemary. Seal the bag and massage the meat with the seasonings through the bag. Store in the fridge for 7 to 10 days, turning the bag over every couple of days to ensure the venison is well coated. If using a vacuum sealer, suck out the air from the bag and store in the fridge for 5 to 7 days. The venison is cured when the meat has become firmer to the touch and when squeezed, it will become darker in colour with visible moisture released by the salt.

Remove the venison from the bag, rinse under cold running water, and pat dry with paper towel. Weigh the venison and record the weight. Hang the cured venison with butcher twine, or place on a wire rack in a wine cooler or fridge set to 50°F (10°C) with the humidity between 60 and 70 percent, and air-dry for 2 weeks.

After hanging for 2 weeks, weigh the venison again. You want the venison to have lost 30 percent of its weight to moisture evaporation. If it hasn't, continue to air-dry the venison until it has lost 30 percent of its weight, up to another 2 weeks. The venison may develop natural, healthy white mould that is safe to eat. Store in an airtight container or wrapped tightly in plastic wrap in the fridge for up to 1 month.

2½ pounds (1.125 kg) venison loin or outside round

¼ cup (60 mL) pure maple syrup

1 tablespoon (15 mL) kosher salt

½ teaspoon (2 mL) curing salt (Prague Powder #1)

1 tablespoon (15 mL) freshly ground juniper berries

4 sprigs fresh thyme

2 sprigs fresh rosemary

The inspiration for this pizza came from my travels to Italy. I was in Positano and ordered a pizza. The only Italian word on the menu I recognized other than pizza was bresaola. I had never had a pizza without sauce, topped only with fresh arugula, Parmesan cheese, freshly shaved cured meat, and a drizzle of olive oil. It was phenomenal. The taste was light and fresh and perfect for a hot summer day. I love making venison bresaola with my deer meat, and this is a perfect way to enjoy it.

VENISON BRESAOLA PIZZA

Makes two 12-inch (30 cm) pizzas

In the bowl of a stand mixer, whisk together the flour, kosher salt, and yeast. Add the warm water, olive oil, and honey. Attach the dough hook and mix on low speed until the dough is smooth and elastic, about 8 minutes.

Remove the bowl from the stand mixer and cover with plastic wrap or a damp kitchen towel. Let the dough rise until it has risen by 50 percent, about 1 hour. This is easier to see when using a glass or clear plastic bowl; use a marker or piece of tape to mark the initial level of the dough.

While the dough is rising, place a pizza stone on the bottom rack of the oven and preheat the oven to 500°F (260°C). (If you do not have a pizza stone, you can use a rimless baking sheet. Note that you will not get the same crispy bottom using a baking sheet.)

Lightly dust a work surface with all-purpose flour. Scrape the dough out onto the floured surface and, using a bench scraper, divide the dough into 2 portions. Shape each portion into a ball. Cover the dough with a damp kitchen towel and let rest for 5 minutes.

Dust 1 portion of the dough with all-purpose flour. Using your hands, stretch the dough into a 12-inch (30 cm) circle. (Alternatively, you can roll out the dough using a rolling pin, but this method will produce a different texture of crust, as the rolling pin will press most of the air out of the dough.) Sprinkle semolina flour and all-purpose flour onto a pizza peel or rimless baking sheet. The flour prevents the dough from sticking and the semolina acts as ball bearings so the dough can slide right off. Place the dough on the peel or baking sheet. Drizzle the dough with olive oil and lightly sprinkle with flaky sea salt. Repeat to assemble the second pizza.

PIZZA DOUGH

3½ cups (875 mL/420 g) unbleached all-purpose flour, more for dusting

1 teaspoon (5 mL) kosher salt

1 packet (¼ ounce/7 g) active dry yeast

1⅓ cups (325 mL) warm water

2 tablespoons (30 mL) olive oil, more for drizzling

1 teaspoon (5 mL) pure liquid honey

Semolina flour, for dusting

Flaky sea salt

TOPPINGS

30 slices shaved Venison Bresaola (page 32)

2 cups (500 mL) loosely packed fresh arugula

⅓-pound (150 g) wedge of Parmesan cheese, shaved

1 teaspoon (5 mL) flaky sea salt

1 bunch fresh basil, leaves only

recipe continues

You will probably need to bake and top one pizza, and then repeat with the second pizza. To transfer the pizza to the stone, place the peel over the stone and quickly pull it back towards you. (Or lift out the hot baking sheet, slide the pizza onto it, and return to the oven.) Bake for 5 to 8 minutes (or 12 to 15 minutes if using a baking sheet), until the dough has crispy edges and golden spots. Use the pizza peel to transfer the pizza to a pizza plate or cutting board. Top each pizza with the shaved venison bresaola, arugula, Parmesan, flaky sea salt, and basil. Slice and serve immediately.

Heart meat is seriously underrated at the dinner table. It is very similar in flavour and texture to a steak or roast but contains more grams of protein than a steak and much less fat. The heart is also a great source of thiamine, folate, selenium, phosphorus, zinc, and several B vitamins. Properly prepared, it is delicious. A classic tartare highlights the flavour of this meat. I've shared a couple of variations below with different preparations and presentations. The venison heart tartare shown on page 39 is served on pickled acorn squash.

VENISON HEART TARTARE

Serves 4

Trim away any fat and silverskin from the outside of the heart. Cut the heart in half lengthwise and cut out and discard any veins or tendons. Dice the cleaned heart meat into ⅛-inch (3 mm) cubes and place in a medium bowl. Add the shallot, capers, mustard, parsley, and a few splashes each of hot sauce and Worcestershire. Add the kosher salt and pepper to taste. Mix until well combined.

Divide the mixture into 4 portions. Place a 3½- to 4-inch (9 to 10 cm) ring mould on a chilled plate and, using a spoon, gently pack the mould with the tartare. Make a small well in the centre of the formed tartare and place a quail egg yolk in the well. Season the yolk with flaky sea salt and freshly cracked pepper. Remove the ring mould. Repeat to assemble the remaining tartares. Serve with fresh artisanal bread or toast.

1 venison heart (about 1 pound/450 g)
1 small shallot, minced
2 tablespoons (30 mL) minced drained capers
1 tablespoon (15 mL) grainy mustard
8 sprigs fresh flat-leaf parsley, chopped
Hot sauce
Worcestershire sauce
½ teaspoon (2 mL) kosher salt
Pinch of freshly ground black pepper
4 quail egg yolks
Flaky sea salt and freshly cracked black pepper
Fresh artisanal bread or toast, for serving

Variation 1

ELK HEART TARTARE

I find elk to be very similar to venison when cooked in a sauce or stew. I assumed that would be the case when eaten raw, but I discovered that raw elk is more complex in flavour. The elk I tasted was shot in southern California, and I was amazed at its flavour compared with elk I had eaten from colder climates. The flavour difference is largely due to the California elk's diet of exotic grasses and bush in the foothills. Prepare using the recipe for Venison Heart Tartare (above).

recipe continues

Variation 2

GARLIC AIOLI

Instead of garnishing the tartare with raw quail yolk, swap it out for this garlic aioli with fresh red currants to give the dish a sweet-and-sour component. Roasting some of the garlic gives the aioli a sweeter, softer garlic taste.

1 head garlic + 2 cloves garlic, divided
1 tablespoon (15 mL) olive oil
1 teaspoon (5 mL) kosher salt
1 large egg
1 tablespoon (15 mL) Dijon mustard
2 cups (500 mL) vegetable oil, divided
Juice of 2 lemons
½ cup (125 mL) fresh red currants, for garnish

Preheat the oven to 400°F (200°C).

Trim about ¼ inch (5 mm) off the top of the head of garlic to expose the cloves, keeping the head intact. Drizzle the olive oil over the exposed cloves. Wrap in foil and roast until the garlic is golden and soft, about 45 minutes. Using a small spoon, extract 5 garlic cloves and squeeze the skin to pop out the roasted garlic. Store the remaining roasted garlic in an airtight container in the fridge for up to 2 weeks or in the freezer for up to 3 months.

Mash the 2 raw garlic cloves with the salt. In a food processor, blend the egg, roasted garlic, mashed garlic, and mustard. With the processor running, very slowly, in a thin stream, pour 1 cup (250 mL) of the vegetable oil through the feed tube. Once the oil is incorporated, add the remaining 1 cup (250 mL) vegetable oil in a steady stream and blend until emulsified. Mix in the lemon juice. Store, covered, in the fridge until ready to use.

Garnish the tartare with a dollop of the garlic aioli and red currants.

Headcheese isn't cheese at all but actually a meat terrine, traditionally made with a whole pig's head. It doesn't include any dairy product whatsoever. This recipe can be used with any animal head, but your pot will need to be larger for larger animals. Despite the terrible branding of the name of this dish, it is delicious, and it's a wonderful way to ensure every bit of the animal is used.

After pulling the meat from the skull, you are also halfway done making a European skull mount, if that is of interest to you. The deer head from making the pictured terrine hangs above the chef's table at the restaurant.

HEADCHEESE

Serves 8 as an appetizer

Line a 8- × 4-inch (1.5 L) loaf pan or terrine mould with 2 layers of plastic wrap, leaving some wrap overhanging the long sides to cover the terrine. Cut a piece of thick cardboard or wood to fit just inside the loaf pan or terrine mould.

Place the head in a pot large enough to hold it comfortably. Add the onion, celery, peppercorns, thyme bunch, bay leaves, and 1 tablespoon (15 mL) of the salt. Add enough water to cover the skull. If you are using a head with antlers, they can stick out of the pot. Bring to a boil, and then reduce to a simmer. Cook, uncovered, until the meat can be easily removed from the skull and cheeks, 3 to 5 hours.

Transfer the head to a large bowl and discard the cooking liquid and vegetables. Let the head sit until the meat is cool enough to handle. Pull the meat from the cheeks and the back of the skull. Remove the tongue and gently peel the outer skin from it; discard the skin. Shred the meat into 1-inch (2.5 cm) chunks. You should have 2 pounds (900 g) cooked meat and tongue. Cover and set aside.

In a small bowl, combine the minced shallots with the white wine vinegar and let macerate for 5 minutes.

In a small saucepan over low heat, melt the duck fat. Add the liquid duck fat to the shredded meat. Add the remaining 2 teaspoons (10 mL) salt, the pepper, chopped thyme, mustard, and macerated shallots and any vinegar. Using your hands, mix thoroughly to combine. Transfer the meat mixture to the loaf pan or terrine mould and pack down the meat mixture. Fold the overhanging plastic wrap over the top to cover. Place the piece of cardboard or wood over the terrine and weigh it down with a couple of heavy cans. Refrigerate overnight before slicing. Store tightly wrapped in plastic wrap in the fridge for up to 1 week.

1 skinned boar, elk, moose, deer, or pig head (about 10 pounds/4.5 kg)

2 cups (500 mL) roughly chopped onion

1 cup (250 mL) roughly chopped celery

2 tablespoons (30 mL) black peppercorns

1 bunch fresh thyme + 1 tablespoon (15 mL) chopped fresh thyme, divided

6 bay leaves

1 tablespoon (15 mL) + 2 teaspoons (10 mL) kosher salt, divided

½ cup (125 mL) minced shallot

¼ cup (60 mL) white wine vinegar

1½ cups (375 mL) rendered duck fat

½ teaspoon (2 mL) freshly ground black pepper

1 tablespoon (15 mL) grainy mustard

Fresh baguette or crackers, sliced pickles, and mustard, for serving

Heart meat is lean and full of flavour, with a texture very similar to beef tenderloin. It is best served rare to medium doneness. Overcooking tends to bring out an unpleasant irony flavour and grainy texture. (Organ meat should be eaten or frozen within a few days of harvesting.)

VENISON HEART STEAK WITH PINE MUSHROOMS, GREEN LENTILS, AND WINTER GREENS

Serves 4

Preheat the oven to 425°F (220°C). Toss the onions with a pinch of salt and 1 tablespoon (15 mL) of the grapeseed oil on a baking sheet. Roast until soft, tender, and sweet, 30 to 45 minutes, stirring halfway through.

Meanwhile, in a small saucepan, combine the vegetable stock, lentils, bay leaves, 1 sprig of the rosemary, chili flakes, 1 tablespoon (15 mL) of the butter, and a pinch each of salt and pepper. Bring to a boil over high heat. Reduce the heat to low, cover, and simmer until all the liquid has been absorbed and the lentils are tender, 15 to 20 minutes. Remove from the heat. Discard the bay leaves and rosemary stems. Cover with a lid and keep warm.

Meanwhile, trim any fat and sinew away from the heart. Trim off the top and bottom tip and discard. Cut the heart horizontally into 4 steaks. Liberally season the heart steaks with salt and pepper. Heat a large cast-iron skillet over high heat until very hot. Add the remaining 1 tablespoon (15 mL) grapeseed oil to the pan and, using tongs so you do not splash yourself with hot oil, carefully place the heart steaks in the pan. Add the remaining sprig of rosemary, crushed garlic, and 1 tablespoon (15 mL) of the butter. Let the meat caramelize for 2 to 3 minutes, then turn and cook for 2 to 3 minutes more for medium-rare doneness. (Caramelizing the meat will give the steak more flavour and a light crust.) Remove the steaks from the pan.

To the hot pan, add the pine mushrooms, the remaining 1 tablespoon (15 mL) butter, and a pinch each of salt and pepper. Sauté until soft and tender and the mushrooms appear wilted, 3 to 5 minutes. Transfer the mushrooms to a bowl. To the same pan, add the Swiss chard, and a pinch of salt and sauté until wilted, about 2 minutes.

To serve, spoon the lentils onto warmed plates. Top with the Swiss chard, steak, mushrooms, and onions.

½ pound (225 g) cipollini onions or pearl onions, peeled

2 tablespoons (30 mL) grapeseed oil or vegetable oil, divided

2 cups (500 mL) vegetable stock

1 cup (250 mL) green or du Puy lentils

2 bay leaves

2 sprigs fresh rosemary, divided

Pinch of red chili flakes

3 tablespoons (45 mL) unsalted butter, divided

Kosher salt and freshly ground black pepper

1 deer heart (about 1 pound/450 g)

4 cloves garlic, crushed

½ pound (225 g) pine mushrooms, brushed clean (oyster mushrooms are a great substitute)

4 cups (1 L) chopped Swiss chard (1 bunch)

We take cuts like the tenderloin for granted because they are so readily available at the grocery store. But when you harvest your own animal, you will truly appreciate just how special the tenderloins are: there are only two tenderloins per animal. Venison tenderloins only weigh 8 to 10 ounces (225 g to 280 g) each roughly the size of a pork tenderloin. The spice ash is a floral and aromatic blend of dark toasted sweet spices that pair wonderfully with venison. Toasting the spices adds depth of flavour and a nutty richness.

VENISON TENDERLOIN WITH SPICE ASH AND CELERIAC PURÉE

Serves 4 to 6

Make the Celeriac Purée

Heat a medium saucepan over medium-low heat. Add the butter and olive oil, then add the celeriac and shallots and cook, stirring frequently, until the vegetables begin to soften, 10 to 15 minutes. Do not let the vegetables brown. Add the garlic, salt, chili flakes, thyme, and bay leaves; stir to combine. Add the white wine and simmer to cook off the alcohol, 2 to 3 minutes. Add the cream and simmer until the cream is partially absorbed and the celeriac is fork-tender, 8 to 10 minutes. Discard the thyme stems and bay leaves. Transfer the celeriac mixture to a high-speed blender or food processor and purée. The purée should be thick and creamy, almost as thick as tomato paste or peanut butter. Reserve in a small pan, covered with a lid, and keep warm until ready to serve. (*The purée can be made ahead and stored in an airtight container in the fridge for up to 5 days.*)

Roast the Squash and Brussels Sprouts

Preheat the oven to 400°F (200°C). Line a baking sheet with parchment paper.

Cut the squash in half lengthwise and scrape out and discard the seeds. Cut the squash halves into 1-inch (2.5 cm) wedges, put them on one side of the prepared baking sheet, and toss with ½ teaspoon (2 mL) each of the salt and pepper. Cut the Brussels sprouts in half and place them on the other side of the baking sheet. Season with the remaining ½ teaspoon (2 mL) each of the salt and pepper. Drizzle the squash and sprouts with the olive oil. Cook until the squash and sprouts are fork-tender and the edges are caramelized, about 30 minutes.

CELERIAC PURÉE

½ cup (125 mL) unsalted butter

1 teaspoon (5 mL) olive oil

1 pound (450 g) celeriac (celery root), peeled and roughly chopped

½ cup (125 mL) sliced shallot

2 tablespoons (30 mL) minced garlic

1 teaspoon (5 mL) kosher salt

½ teaspoon (2 mL) red chili flakes

2 sprigs fresh thyme

2 bay leaves

1 cup (250 mL) dry white wine

1 cup (250 mL) heavy (35%) cream

ROASTED SQUASH AND BRUSSELS SPROUTS

1 acorn squash

1 teaspoon (5 mL) kosher salt, divided

1 teaspoon (5 mL) freshly ground black pepper, divided

1 pound (450 g) Brussels sprouts, trimmed

2 tablespoons (30 mL) olive oil

Cook the Venison Tenderloin with Spice Ash

Season the tenderloins with sea salt and pepper, then roll in the Spice Ash until evenly coated. Heat a cast-iron or other heavy skillet over high heat. Add the butter and olive oil and sear the tenderloins on all sides, 1 minute per side for medium-rare doneness. Remove from the pan and let rest for 3 to 4 minutes before slicing.

Serve the tenderloin on top of the celeriac purée, with the roasted squash and Brussels sprouts.

VENISON TENDERLOIN WITH SPICE ASH

2 venison tenderloins (8 to 10 ounces/225 g to 280 g each)

Sea salt and black pepper

3 tablespoons (45 mL) Spice Ash (page 73)

3 tablespoons (45 mL) unsalted butter, for searing

1 tablespoon (15 mL) olive oil, for searing

Elk is very similar to venison—very lean and with comparable flavour, although the meat will always taste different depending on the diet of the animal and where it came from. An elk in the western part of North America is going to be eating and living in different conditions than an elk in the eastern part of North America. Nonetheless, it has a rich earthy flavour that is delicious. Because of the low fat content, elk roasts are best cooked low and slow with lots of aromatics. I like to tie my roasts with herbs and sear in a cast-iron pan for flavour, then transfer to the oven to very slowly cook to medium-rare.

ELK ROAST WITH HARVEST VEGETABLES

Serves 6

Preheat the oven to 325°F (160°C).

Truss the roast with butcher twine and season with salt and pepper. Heat the grapeseed oil in a large cast-iron skillet over medium-high heat. Sear the meat on all sides, 1 to 2 minutes per side. Remove the roast from the pan. To the hot pan, add the Brussels sprouts, radishes, potatoes, shallots, carrots, rosemary, and bay leaves, and drizzle the melted butter over the vegetables. Place the elk on top of the vegetables and transfer to the oven. Cook until the internal temperature reaches 125°F (50°C) for medium-rare doneness, 15 to 20 minutes. Remove the elk from the oven and continue roasting the vegetables until fork-tender. Discard the rosemary stems and bay leaves. Let the elk rest for at least 5 to 10 minutes before slicing. Cover with foil to keep warm. Serve with the roasted vegetables.

3 pounds (1.35 kg) elk striploin, inside round, or outside round

1 tablespoon (15 mL) kosher salt

1½ teaspoons (7 mL) freshly cracked black pepper

1 tablespoon (15 mL) grapeseed oil or vegetable oil

½ pound (225 g) Brussels sprouts, cut in half

½ pound (225 g) radishes, cut in half

½ pound (225 g) baby potatoes

½ pound (225 g) shallots or pearl onions, peeled

½ pound (225 g) heirloom carrots, peeled

1 bunch fresh rosemary

4 bay leaves

1 tablespoon (15 mL) melted unsalted butter

Venison shanks are a wonderful cut when cooked properly. A long, gentle braise will soften the meat and release that marrow flavour from the bone. You can cut the shanks horizontally with a hacksaw or reciprocating saw, so they resemble osso buco. This way they'll cook faster, and the exposed marrow will be easy to scoop out with a spoon while eating. The potato purée is glorified mashed potatoes, with more butter, cream, and cheddar cheese.

BRAISED VENISON SHANKS WITH POTATO PURÉE AND TOMATO JAM

Serves 4

Make the Tomato Jam

In a medium saucepan, heat the olive oil over medium heat. Add the tomatoes and cook until softened, 3 to 5 minutes. Add the shallots, garlic, chili pepper, salt, and black pepper to taste, stir to combine, and cook for another 5 minutes. Reduce the heat to low, add the thyme, bay leaves, brown sugar, and sherry vinegar and cook until a thick jam consistency, stirring occasionally to keep the bottom from burning, 10 to 15 minutes. Remove from the heat. The jam can be served warm or at room temperature. Discard the bay leaves and thyme stems before serving. Store in an airtight container in the fridge for up to 1 week. Gently reheat if desired.

Braise the Venison Shanks

Preheat the oven to 350°F (180°C).

Season the shanks with 1½ teaspoons (7 mL) of the salt and 1 teaspoon (5 mL) of the pepper. Heat a large lidded pot over high heat. Add the grapeseed oil to the pot. Sear the shanks on all sides to caramelize the meat to a deep brown colour. Transfer the shanks to a plate. Add the onion, carrot, celery, and garlic to the pot and cook the vegetables over high heat, stirring occasionally, until browned, 5 to 6 minutes. Deglaze with the red wine.

Put the shanks and any juices back in the pot. Add the tomatoes and their juice, stock, thyme, rosemary, bay leaves, chili flakes, and the remaining 1½ teaspoons (7 mL) salt and 1 teaspoon (5 mL) pepper. Bring to a boil. Cover with a lid, transfer to the oven, and braise until the meat

TOMATO JAM

¼ cup (60 mL) olive oil

1 pound (450 g) Roma tomatoes, chopped

½ cup (125 mL) finely chopped shallot

¼ cup (60 mL) minced garlic

1 tablespoon (15 mL) minced fresh chili pepper

1 teaspoon (5 mL) kosher salt

Freshly ground black pepper

4 sprigs fresh thyme

2 bay leaves

½ cup (125 mL) brown sugar

3 tablespoons (45 mL) sherry vinegar

BRAISED VENISON SHANKS

3 pounds (1.35 kg) bone-in venison shanks (about 2 shanks)

3 teaspoons (15 mL) kosher salt, divided

2 teaspoons (10 mL) freshly ground black pepper, divided

recipe and ingredients continues

can be easily pulled from the bone, about 3 hours. If the stew is loose, you can simmer it gently with the meat to reduce and thicken. Discard the thyme and rosemary stems and the bay leaves before serving.

Make the Potato Purée

In a large saucepan, cover the potatoes with cold water and add 1 tablespoon (15 mL) of the salt. Simmer the potatoes over medium heat until fork-tender, 20 to 30 minutes. Drain the potatoes, then mash with a potato masher. Using a whisk, whip in the warm cream, melted butter, cheese, and the remaining 1 teaspoon (5 mL) salt. The purée should be thick and spreadable with a spoon.

To serve, spread the potato purée in deep plates, top with the venison shanks with the reduced stew, and spoon the tomato jam on top. Garnish with chopped fresh rosemary and thyme.

Tip Whole potatoes take longer to cook but will not absorb as much water and will retain more flavour. Starting potatoes in cold water allows them to heat gradually so they cook more evenly. Putting them in boiling water overcooks the outside before the inside is soft.

2 tablespoons (30 mL) grapeseed or vegetable oil, for frying

1 cup (250 mL) diced white onion

½ cup (125 mL) diced carrot

½ cup (125 mL) diced celery

6 cloves garlic, crushed

1 cup (250 mL) dry red wine

1 can (28 ounces/796 mL) diced tomatoes

4 cups (1 L) Venison Stock (page 70) or beef stock

½ bunch fresh thyme, more for garnish

4 sprigs fresh rosemary, more for garnish

2 bay leaves

½ teaspoon (2 mL) red chili flakes

POTATO PURÉE

4 large Yukon Gold or white potatoes (about 1¾ pounds/790 g), peeled

1 tablespoon (15 mL) + 1 teaspoon (5 mL) kosher salt, divided

½ cup (125 mL) heavy (35%) cream, warmed

½ cup (125 mL) unsalted butter, melted

½ cup (125 mL) grated white cheddar cheese

Wild boar is very similar to pork in texture and taste. It tends to be leaner and has a darker colour with a subtle gamey flavour depending on the diet of the animal. Boars in the wild are much leaner and gamier tasting than farm-raised breeds. This recipe can be made using a centre-cut bone-in roast, or you can replace the wild boar chops with good-quality organic pork chops.

ROASTED WILD BOAR LOIN CHOPS WITH CRANBERRY APPLE MOSTARDA AND GRAINY MUSTARD SPÄTZLE

Serves 4

Brine the Wild Boar Loin Chops

In a small saucepan, combine the water, salt, garlic, thyme, and bay leaves and bring to a boil over high heat. Remove from the heat and let cool to room temperature. Put the boar chops in a large plastic container. Pour the brine over the chops, cover, and refrigerate for at least 4 hours or overnight to allow flavours to meld.

Make the Mostarda

In a small saucepan, heat the grapeseed oil over medium heat. Add the onion, cinnamon stick, star anise, and cardamom and cook, stirring occasionally, until the onion is soft and translucent, about 5 minutes. Add the apples, dried cranberries, sugar, apple cider vinegar, and mustard seeds. Continue cooking, stirring occasionally, until all the liquid has evaporated. Stir in the mustard oil and remove from the heat. Remove the whole spices and discard. The mostarda can be served warm or at room temperature.

Make the Spätzle

In a medium bowl using a wooden spoon, mix together the flour, milk, eggs, mustard, thyme, salt, and nutmeg. (Alternatively, you can use a stand mixer fitted with the paddle attachment and beat on low to medium speed for 3 to 4 minutes.) The mixture should form a thick, glutinous paste.

Bring a large pot of salted water to a boil over high heat.

Using the back of a ladle, push the dough through a colander into the boiling water. Cook until the noodles float to the surface, 2 to 3 minutes. Scoop out the noodles using a slotted spoon or sieve and cool slightly on a baking sheet.

ROASTED WILD BOAR LOIN CHOPS

2 cups (500 mL) water

2 tablespoons (30 mL) kosher salt

4 cloves garlic, crushed

4 sprigs fresh thyme

4 bay leaves

4 bone-in centre-cut boar loin chops or pork chops (10 ounces/280 g each)

2 tablespoons (30 mL) grapeseed oil or vegetable oil, for searing

CRANBERRY APPLE MOSTARDA

1 tablespoon (15 mL) grapeseed oil or vegetable oil

1 cup (250 mL) diced white onion

1 cinnamon stick (or ½ teaspoon/2 mL ground cinnamon)

1 star anise (or ¼ teaspoon/1 mL ground star anise)

4 green cardamom pods (or ¼ teaspoon/1 mL ground cardamom)

recipe and ingredients continues

Roast the Chops and Pan-Fry the Spätzle

Remove the chops from the brine, discarding the brine, and pat dry with paper towel. It is important to dry the meat well so you are not cooking wet meat. Heat a large cast-iron or other heavy skillet over high heat. Add the grapeseed oil, then, using tongs, place the chops in the pan. Reduce the heat to medium-low and cook the chops for 5 to 6 minutes per side, turning once. The chops should have a golden brown crust on both sides. I like to cook the chops to medium doneness, with an internal temperature of 135°F (58°C). If you prefer them more well done, finish the chops in the oven at 325°F (160°C) to avoid overcooking the outside on the burner.

When the chops are done, heat a large seasoned or nonstick frying pan over medium-high heat, then add the vegetable oil. Add the spätzle and let them crisp on the bottom, without moving them, 2 to 3 minutes. Toss or stir, then cook for 1 minute more. The spätzle should be lightly crisp on the outside and soft on the inside.

To serve, spoon the fried spätzle onto warmed plates. Place a chop on top of the spätzle and finish with the cranberry apple mostarda.

Tips If you don't have time to wait for the brine to cool, use just 1 cup (250 mL) of water in the boiled brine mixture. After boiling the brine, add 1 cup (250 mL) of ice cubes to cool the brine instantly.

A brine can also be used for chicken, turkey, duck, goose, and any other game birds with a variety of spices and herbs. Have fun and experiment. My recipe for brine is 7 percent salinity in water by weight. For example, a brine of 4 cups (1 L) water would require ¼ cup (60 mL) salt.

Mustard oil can be found in health food stores and South Asian grocery stores.

You can make the spätzle using a spätzle maker. They are available in kitchen stores and online.

2 large Honeycrisp apples (or Mutsu, Gala, or Granny Smith), peeled and diced

½ cup (125 mL) dried cranberries

½ cup (125 mL) granulated sugar

¼ cup (60 mL) apple cider vinegar

1 tablespoon (15 mL) yellow mustard seeds

2 tablespoons (30 mL) mustard oil

GRAINY MUSTARD SPÄTZLE

1 cup (250 mL) all-purpose flour

¼ cup (60 mL) whole milk

2 large eggs

1 tablespoon (15 mL) grainy mustard

2 teaspoons (10 mL) chopped fresh thyme

½ teaspoon (2 mL) kosher salt

⅛ teaspoon (0.5 mL) nutmeg

1 tablespoon (15 mL) vegetable oil, for frying

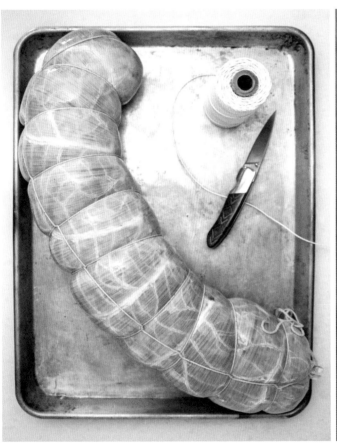
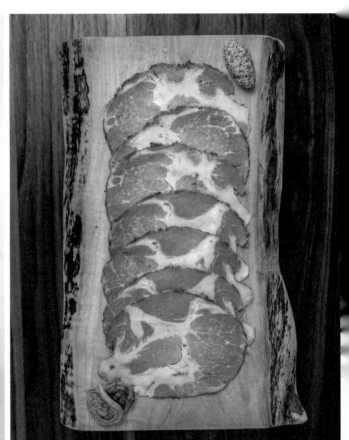

Capicola is a dry-cured Italian-style sausage or ham, using either whole muscle from the neck, called the pork butt, or, as in this recipe, large chunks of cured meat. The meat is hand-stuffed into a casing and hung to dry. The sausage has a rich, succulent, slightly salty flavour and is marbled with fat. It can be prepared either sweet or spicy. Wild boar capicola makes a great addition to any charcuterie board or in a sandwich paired with any sharp aged cheese.

To prepare this dry cured delicacy, I use large whole chunks of meat held together by a large intestine called a beef middle or cap end. Ask your local butcher or charcuterie shop to sell you the cap end casing (also called beef bung casing) and curing salt. Intestines come from the butcher packed in curing salt and must be soaked and rinsed before use. Synthetic casing and curing salt are also available online.

You will need a hygrometer to measure the humidity. They are available in hardware stores and online.

WILD BOAR CAPICOLA

Makes about 1¾ pounds (790 g) dry-cured meat

In a large bowl, combine the wild boar, kosher salt, curing salt, sugar, paprika and cayenne pepper (if using), black pepper, juniper, bay leaves, and thyme. Mix thoroughly with your hands, massaging the dry ingredients into the meat.

Place the boar mixture in a large thick resealable plastic bag or vacuum bag. Seal the bag and refrigerate for 7 to 10 days, turning the bag over every couple of days to ensure the meat is well coated. If using a vacuum sealer, suck out the air from the bag and store in the fridge for 5 to 7 days. The boar is cured when the meat has become firmer to the touch and when squeezed, it will become darker in colour and visible moisture will be released by the salt.

Soak and rinse the intestine in a medium bowl of cold water for 30 minutes to remove the salts and soften the casing. Follow package directions for synthetic casings.

Remove the wild boar from the plastic bag and pat dry with paper towel. Use your hands to fill the casing with the boar. Tie the top with butcher twine, then truss or make individual ties every inch (2.5 cm) down the sausage to push out any air pockets. If you notice big air bubbles, prick them with a wooden skewer. Weigh the sausage and record the weight.

Hang the sausage with butcher twine in a wine cooler, cold cellar or fridge set to 50°F (10°C) with the humidity between 60 and 70 percent, and air-dry for about 1 month. The capicola is finished when it has lost 30 percent of its weight to moisture evaporation.

2½ pounds (1.125 kg) wild boar or pork shoulder, cut into large chunks

½ cup (125 mL) kosher or sea salt (I use Diamond Crystal)

½ teaspoon (2 mL) curing salt (Prague Powder #1)

1 tablespoon (15 mL) granulated sugar

1 tablespoon (15 mL) hot paprika (optional)

1 teaspoon (5 mL) cayenne pepper (optional)

2 teaspoons (10 mL) freshly ground black pepper

½ teaspoon (2 mL) ground juniper berries

3 bay leaves

1 sprig fresh thyme

3 feet (1 m) beef middle, or cap end, intestine (or synthetic casing)

A Christmas Eve tourtière somehow worked itself into my family traditions even though my family is not French-Canadian. I will happily continue to pass on the tradition because this is one of my all-time favourite dishes. The richness of the meat and the flavour of game combined with fatty, flaky pastry is pure bliss, especially during the winter months. I like to serve this with a sweet-and-sour chutney or Wild Grape Coulis (page 65).

GAME TOURTIÈRE

Serves 6

Make the Butter Pastry Dough

In the bowl of a stand mixer fitted with the paddle attachment, combine the flour, butter, lard, and salt. Mix on low speed until the mixture has just formed into a paste. Do not overmix. Add the water and mix on low speed just until incorporated. Do not overmix. Overmixing will cause the pastry to be tough and crunchy, not supple and flaky.

Turn the dough out onto a work surface and divide into 2 portions, with 1 portion slightly larger than the other. Press each portion of dough flat onto a sheet of plastic wrap, fold half the wrap overtop, and shape each portion into a ½-inch (1 cm) thick disc. Wrap tightly and refrigerate for at least 1 hour and ideally overnight. This allows the gluten in the dough to relax, making it easier to roll out with less shrinkage.

Make the Filling

Heat a medium pot over high heat. Add the grapeseed oil, boar, venison, and duck and cook, stirring occasionally, until the meat is browned, 6 to 8 minutes. Reduce the heat to medium, then add the butter, onion, mushrooms, potato, cinnamon, cloves, juniper, chili flakes, and cayenne. Cook, stirring occasionally, until the onions are soft and translucent, about 5 minutes. Deglaze with the white wine, scraping the bottom with a wooden spoon, and cook until the wine has evaporated. Add the bacon and garlic, and stir to combine. Remove from the heat and let cool to room temperature before filling the pie shell.

BUTTER PASTRY DOUGH

3¼ cups (810 mL/390 g) all-purpose flour, more for dusting

¾ cup (175 mL/170 g) unsalted butter, at room temperature

¼ cup (60 mL/55 g) lard, at room temperature

1 teaspoon (5 mL/5 g) kosher salt

⅓ cup + 1 tablespoon (100 mL/100 g) cold water

2 beaten egg yolks, for egg wash

FILLING

2 tablespoons (30 mL) grapeseed oil or vegetable oil, for frying

½ pound (225 g) ground wild boar

½ pound (225 g) ground venison

½ pound (225 g) ground duck

½ cup (125 mL) unsalted butter

1 cup (250 mL) diced white onion

¼ pound (115 g) wild mushrooms, sliced (chanterelles or oyster mushrooms are good substitutes)

recipe and ingredients continues

Assemble and Bake the Tourtière

Preheat the oven to 425°F (220°C).

Let the wrapped dough rest on a work surface for 20 to 30 minutes before rolling. If the dough is too cold it will crack; if it is at room temperature it will be too sticky and will not hold together properly. Remove the plastic wrap and lightly flour the top of the larger disc of dough. On a lightly floured work surface, gently roll out the dough into a 12-inch (30 cm) circle about ⅛ inch (3 mm) thick. Loosely roll the dough over the rolling pin and transfer the pastry to a deep 9-inch (23 cm) pie plate. Gently press the dough into the pan and trim the edges flush with the pan. Roll out the smaller piece of dough for the top of the tourtière.

Using a fork, gently prick the bottom of the pie shell multiple times in 1-inch (2.5 cm) increments. These small indents in the pastry will allow steam to escape and keep the pastry from rising. Scrape the meat filling into the pie shell and gently pat down. Brush the rim of the pastry with the egg wash. Carefully transfer the top layer of pastry onto the pie. Pinch the edges of the dough together to create a wavy pattern and seal the edges, or press with a fork around the edge to seal the top layer of pastry to the pie. Brush the top of the pie with the egg wash. Cut an X in the middle of the pie and randomly prick a few holes with a fork to allow steam to escape during baking. If you like, make decorations with scrap pieces of pastry.

Bake the pie for 5 minutes. Reduce the oven temperature to 350°F (180°C) and bake for 1 to 1½ hours longer. The crust should be a deep golden brown. Transfer the pie to a rack and let rest for 15 to 20 minutes before cutting and serving.

Tip When preparing the butter pastry dough, for best results use a digital scale and prepare the pastry the day before.

1 cup (250 mL) peeled and grated white potato
1 tablespoon (15 mL) cinnamon
1 teaspoon (5 mL) ground cloves
1 teaspoon (5 mL) ground juniper berries
½ teaspoon (2 mL) red chili flakes
½ teaspoon (2 mL) cayenne pepper
1 cup (250 mL) dry white wine
¼ pound (115 g) Wild Boar Bacon (page 87) or fatback, diced
4 teaspoons (20 mL) minced garlic

When I helped cook for a charity event for Catch-A-Dream Foundation and St. Jude Children's Research Hospital in Mississippi, I was paired up with a bunch of barbecue chefs from Nashville, Tennessee. It was from them I learned how to dry-smoke ribs. Once you truly nail a dry rub and master smoking ribs, I doubt you will ever go back to braised ribs again. The flavour is far superior. A great accompaniment is my Maple Baked Beans (page 115).

BARBECUED VENISON AND WILD BOAR RIBS

Serves 4 to 6

Place the boar and venison ribs on a baking sheet. In a small bowl, combine the brown sugar, paprika, salt, pepper, and thyme. Using your hands, cover the meat evenly on both sides with the dry rub. Massage the rub into the meat. Cover with plastic wrap and refrigerate for at least 4 hours or overnight to marinate.

For the best-tasting results, I recommend using a smoker set to 300°F (150°C), but you can roast the ribs in the oven at the same temperature using the same method. Put the baking sheet in the smoker or oven, add the water to the pan, and cook the ribs, basting with the pan drippings after the first hour, then every 30 minutes. Dry-roasting or smoking usually takes about 3 hours, but depending on the thickness of the ribs, you will want to start checking their doneness after 2 hours and then every 30 minutes. Tug at a bone on the end of the rack. If it is rubbery and not pulling apart easily, it is not done. Ribs with a dry rub will never be quite as tender as braised ribs, so do not expect the meat to fall off the bone. Let the ribs rest for 5 to 10 minutes before slicing and serving.

4 pounds (1.8 kg) wild boar back ribs or pork ribs

4 pounds (1.8 kg) venison ribs

¼ cup (60 mL) brown sugar

¼ cup (60 mL) hot paprika

1 tablespoon (15 mL) kosher salt or sea salt

2 teaspoons (10 mL) freshly ground black pepper

4 sprigs fresh thyme, leaves only, chopped

1 cup (250 mL) water

Tip For even juicier ribs, brine the ribs overnight before marinating with the dry rub. See page 93 for a basic brine recipe.

Liver is a love-or-hate type of food for many people. If you are a fan, you will love this dish. When I harvest an animal, the first thing I eat is the offal. The liver is a great source of high-quality protein and is one of the most concentrated sources of vitamin A, along with folic acid and iron. When prepared correctly it is delicious. The onions add a touch of sweetness that pairs nicely with the earthy flavour of the liver, while the tartness of the wild grapes cuts the meat's richness. The Wild Grape Coulis makes a nice accompaniment to many other game dishes or cheese plates.

PAN-FRIED VENISON LIVER WITH WILD GRAPE COULIS

Serves 4

Make the Wild Grape Coulis

In a medium saucepan, crush the grapes lightly with a potato masher or the bottom of a ladle to release some of the liquid. Add the sugar and cook, stirring frequently, over medium heat until the sauce has thickened enough to coat the back of a spoon, about 15 minutes. Remove from the heat. *(The coulis can be made ahead and stored in an airtight container in the fridge for up to 1 week.)*

Prepare the Venison Liver

Slice the venison liver horizontally into 4 equal portions and place in a plastic container. Pour the milk over the liver, cover, and let soak overnight in the fridge. This tenderizes the liver and removes some of the gamey and irony taste.

Make the Caramelized Onions

In a medium skillet, heat the grapeseed oil over high heat for 1 minute. Add the onions and thyme, reduce the heat to medium, cover with a lid, and cook, stirring frequently, until the onions are completely soft, 20 to 30 minutes. You will notice that a lot of liquid is released from the onions. When the onions are soft and translucent, add the brandy and sugar. Increase the heat to high and cook, uncovered and stirring frequently to avoid burning, for 3 to 5 minutes. This is to reduce the natural water from the onions and caramelize the sugar. When the pot has become dry, the onions will start to turn colour. When the onions are a deep golden brown, appear completely mushy, and taste very sweet, they are done. Remove from the heat.

WILD GRAPE COULIS

1 pound (450 g) wild grapes, stemmed (Champagne grapes or fresh red currants are good alternatives)

2 cups (500 mL) granulated sugar

PAN-FRIED VENISON LIVER

1 pound (450 g) venison liver or calf's liver

2 cups (500 mL) whole milk

Kosher salt or sea salt

Freshly ground black pepper

2 tablespoons (30 mL) grapeseed oil or vegetable oil, for frying

CARAMELIZED ONIONS

1 tablespoon (15 mL) grapeseed oil or vegetable oil, for cooking

4 cups (1 L) thinly sliced white onion (about 2 large Spanish onions)

recipe and ingredients continues

Fry the Venison Liver

Remove the liver from the milk, discarding the milk, and pat dry with paper towel. Season both sides of the liver with a generous pinch each of salt and pepper. Heat a large cast-iron or other heavy skillet over high heat. Add the grapeseed oil to the pan. Using tongs, place the liver in the pan and fry for 1 to 2 minutes per side for rare doneness. For the best-tasting results, I recommend eating the liver rare or medium-rare.

Serve the liver with a spoonful of the caramelized onions on top and a spoonful of the wild grape coulis around the liver.

2 sprigs fresh thyme, leaves only, chopped
½ cup (125 mL) brandy
1 tablespoon (15 mL) granulated sugar

This dish is my take on classic Parisian steak-frites, using game meat, of course. Venison, moose, or elk can be used in place of bison. I like to use pine mushrooms mainly because they grow during the hunting season and happen to grow underneath my deer stand, but you can use any mushrooms you like. Some good choices are chanterelles or oyster mushrooms.

For this recipe, you will need a deep-fry thermometer to check the temperature of the oil. If the oil gets too hot, it may catch fire.

BISON RIBEYE WITH TRUFFLE PARMESAN FRITES, PINE MUSHROOMS, AND MADEIRA JUS

Serves 4

Half-fill a large pot with the canola oil and heat it to 300°F (150°C).

Wash the potatoes and cut lengthwise into 3-inch (8 cm) batons. Carefully add the cut potatoes to the hot oil using tongs, a small sieve, or a fryer basket. Blanch the potatoes for 1 to 2 minutes, until the potatoes are cooked through but not yet turning colour. Using tongs (or basket, if using), transfer the fries to a sieve or colander over a bowl to drain. Let the potatoes cool to room temperature while you prepare the steaks.

In a small saucepan, combine the reduced venison stock and Madeira. Bring to a simmer over medium heat and reduce until the sauce coats the back of a spoon, about 5 minutes. Taste for seasoning and adjust with salt, if needed. Remove from the heat and keep warm.

Increase the temperature of the oil to 350°F (180°C). You will use this oil to finish frying the fries after cooking the steak.

Season the bison ribeye steaks with salt and pepper. Heat a large cast-iron or other heavy skillet over high heat until the pan is smoking hot, 3 to 5 minutes. Add 1 tablespoon (15 mL) canola oil. Using tongs, place the steaks in the pan and sear each side for 2 to 3 minutes for medium-rare doneness, internal temperature 125°F (50°C). Transfer the steaks to a rack and let rest. Add the pine mushrooms and a pinch of salt to the same pan and sauté in the steak juices until wilted, 2 to 3 minutes. Remove from the heat.

About 8 cups (2 L) + 1 tablespoon (15 mL) canola oil, for frying, divided

1½ pounds (675 g) unpeeled white potatoes (about 3 large potatoes; russets are best)

½ cup (125 mL) reduced Venison Stock (page 70)

2 tablespoons (30 mL) sweet Madeira

Kosher salt or sea salt

4 bison ribeye steaks (8 ounces/225 g each)

Freshly ground black pepper

½ pound (225 g) pine mushrooms, brushed clean and cut in half

2 tablespoons (30 mL) freshly grated Parmesan cheese

1 teaspoon (5 mL) fresh thyme leaves (from about 1 sprig)

1 tablespoon (15 mL) truffle oil (or a generous shaving of fresh truffle)

recipe continues

Meanwhile, return the fries to the hot oil and cook until deep golden, 3 to 4 minutes. Using tongs (or basket, if using), transfer the fries to a colander, shaking to remove excess oil. Transfer the fries to a medium bowl and toss with salt, pepper, Parmesan, thyme, and truffle oil.

To serve, place the steaks on plates. Spoon the mushrooms on top of the steaks and pile the fries beside the steaks. Spoon the Madeira jus over the mushrooms and steaks.

Stock is a flavourful fundamental base for soups, sauces, and braising liquids and can be used in many recipes in your home kitchen. A good stock is nutrient-rich and makes your house smell wonderful while it simmers away. There are a few different types of stock that you can experiment with. A clear, or light, stock is one where the bones are simply simmered without roasting first with vegetables and aromatic herbs for several hours; it is used to make clear or white soups or sauces or for braising white meats or fish. A dark, or brown, stock is made by first roasting the bones to give them a caramelized flavour and appearance; it is used for braising red meats or making dark sauces and reductions. For a fish or clear white stock, omit the tomato and carrot, and replace the red wine with white wine. This recipe is for a dark venison stock, but you can substitute the bones of beef, pork, wild boar, elk, turkey, and so on.

VENISON STOCK

Makes 2½ gallons (10 L)

Preheat the oven to 400°F (200°C).

Spread the venison bones in a large roasting pan. Transfer to the oven and roast the bones for about 45 minutes or until dark brown. Transfer the bones to a large stockpot.

To the roasting pan, add the onion, carrot, and celery and stir with a wooden spoon. Roast the vegetables until they begin to caramelize, about 15 minutes. Transfer the vegetables to the stockpot. Deglaze the roasting pan with the red wine, scraping any caramelized bits off the bottom with a wooden spoon. Pour the wine into the stockpot. Add the tomatoes and their juice, thyme, rosemary, bay leaves, and peppercorns. Add enough cold water to cover the bones and vegetables. Bring to a boil over high heat, then reduce the heat and cook the stock at a light simmer, uncovered, for 6 to 8 hours or overnight. (Skim off any foam or fat if making a clear broth or consommé.) Do not stir the stock. Stirring will cause the vegetables to break down instead of simply extracting their flavour and will result in a cloudy, murky appearance and muddled flavour.

Remove from the heat and let cool slightly. Strain the stock by carefully tipping the pot and pouring the liquid through a fine-mesh strainer into another large pot. Discard the solids. Allow the liquid to settle for a few minutes, then use a ladle to skim off the fat floating on top. Portion the stock into 4-cup (1 L) containers and store in the fridge for up to 1 week or in the freezer for up to 1 year.

8 pounds (3.5 kg) meaty venison bones (shanks, hips, spine)

4 cups (1 L) roughly chopped Spanish onion (about 4 onions)

2 cups (500 mL) roughly chopped carrot (about 2 carrots)

2 cups (500 mL) roughly chopped celery (about 2 stalks celery)

1 bottle (26 ounces/750 mL) dry red wine

1 can (28 ounces/796 mL) whole tomatoes

½ bunch fresh thyme

½ bunch fresh rosemary

6 bay leaves

1 tablespoon (15 mL) black peppercorns

The venison rack is the part of the deer I prize the most. After harvesting my first deer, I learned just how special this cut is when I realized how little of the rack there was compared with how much secondary meat is on the animal. The primal cuts of the ribs, tenderloin, and striploin make up a very small portion of the total usable meat on an animal. I usually make four frenched racks from a rib cage. This dish perfectly shows how you can use different parts of the animal on one plate. The neck meat is one of my favourite cuts of the deer. There is a lot of marbling and fatty connective tissue between all the bones. The meat is melt-in-your-mouth tender when braised and full of flavour. The pairing of rare cooked venison with the braised meat goes together perfectly.

ROAST VENISON RACK AND NECK RAGOUT WITH SPICE ASH AND PARSNIP PURÉE

Serves 6 to 8

Make the Spice Ash

Set a rack in the bottom of the oven and preheat the broiler. In a medium skillet, one at a time, toast the coriander seeds, juniper berries, star anise, cloves, allspice, cardamom pods, and cinnamon sticks under the broiler, tossing the spices in the pan every minute. (Alternatively, you can toast the spices, one at a time, on the stove over medium heat, shaking the pan occasionally to ensure even toasting. Be careful as the pan will be very hot.) The spices will give off smoke, so make sure the exhaust fan is on high. When the spices are evenly blackened, transfer to a stainless steel or heat-tempered glass bowl (do not use plastic). Once slightly cooled, combine all the toasted spices in a food processor and pulse until a fine powder. Sift the spices through a fine-mesh sieve to remove any larger gritty pieces; discard them or blend again to break down more. Once the spice ash powder is cool, store it in an airtight jar at room temperature for up to 3 months.

Make the Venison Neck Ragout

Preheat the oven to 350°F (180°C).

Season the venison neck with 1½ teaspoons (7 mL) of the salt and 1 teaspoon (5 mL) of the pepper. Heat a large pot over high heat. Add the grapeseed oil to the pan, then add the neck and sear on all sides to caramelize the meat to a deep brown colour. Transfer the neck to a plate. Reduce the heat to medium and add the onion, carrot, and celery to the pot. Cook the vegetables, stirring occasionally, until caramelized. Deglaze with the red wine. Put the neck and any juices back in the pot. Add the

SPICE ASH (MAKES EXTRA)
¼ cup (60 mL) coriander seeds
¼ cup (60 mL) juniper berries
¼ cup (60 mL) whole star anise
¼ cup (60 mL) whole cloves
¼ cup (60 mL) whole allspice
¼ cup (60 mL) green cardamom
    pods
8 cinnamon sticks

VENISON NECK RAGOUT
3 pounds (1.35 kg) bone-in
    venison neck
3 teaspoons (15 mL) kosher salt,
    divided
2 teaspoons (10 mL) freshly
    ground black pepper, divided
3 tablespoons (45 mL)
    grapeseed oil or vegetable oil,
    for frying
1 cup (250 mL) diced white onion
½ cup (125 mL) diced carrot
½ cup (125 mL) diced celery
1 cup (250 mL) dry red wine

recipe and ingredients continues

tomatoes, venison stock, garlic, thyme, rosemary, bay leaves, chili flakes, the remaining 1½ teaspoons (7 mL) salt, and the remaining 1 teaspoon (5 mL) pepper. Bring to a boil. Cover with a lid and transfer to the oven. Braise until the meat can be easily pulled from the bone, 3 to 4 hours.

Remove the pot from the oven (keep the oven on). Remove the neck from the pot and shred the meat from the bone using tongs and a fork. Return the meat to the braising liquid. If the stew is loose, simmer it gently with the pulled meat to reduce and thicken. Set aside and keep warm.

Make the Parsnip Purée

Heat a medium saucepan over medium-low heat. Add the butter, parsnips, and shallots and cook, stirring frequently, until soft, 10 to 15 minutes. Do not let the parsnips colour. Add the garlic, salt, chili flakes, thyme, and bay leaves and stir to combine. Add the white wine and cook to boil off the alcohol, stirring occasionally to avoid burning the bottom, 2 to 3 minutes. Then add the cream and simmer over low heat until the cream is fully reduced and absorbed, 8 to 10 minutes. Remove from the heat.

Discard the thyme stems and bay leaves. Scoop out the parsnips and transfer to a food processor or high-speed blender. Blend until the purée is thick and creamy, almost as thick as tomato paste or peanut butter. Return the purée to the saucepan, cover, and keep warm until ready to serve. (*The purée can be made ahead and stored in an airtight container in the fridge for up to 5 days.*)

Cook the Rack of Venison

The oven should already be preheated at 350°F (180°C).

Truss the rack of venison using butcher twine. This will keep the meat tight to the bone and it will cook more evenly. Season with salt and pepper and rub generously with the spice ash.

Heat a large skillet over high heat and add the grapeseed oil. Place the rack in the pan and sear on all sides, 1 to 2 minutes per side. Transfer the skillet to the oven. Racks will cook at different times depending on their size. Use a probe thermometer to check the internal temperature of the meat after 6 to 8 minutes. For a beautifully rare centre, remove from the oven when the thermometer reaches 120°F (50°C). Let rest for about 7 minutes before slicing into chops.

To serve, scoop a large spoonful of parsnip purée onto a plate, make a well in the centre with the bottom of a spoon, and fill with the ragout. Place a venison rack chop on top.

1 can (28 ounces/796 mL) diced tomatoes

4 cups (1 L) Venison Stock (page 70) or beef stock

6 cloves garlic, crushed

½ bunch fresh thyme

4 sprigs fresh rosemary

2 bay leaves

½ teaspoon (2 mL) red chili flakes

PARSNIP PURÉE

½ cup (125 mL) unsalted butter

1 pound (450 g) parsnips, peeled and thinly sliced

½ cup (125 mL) sliced shallot

2 tablespoons (30 mL) minced garlic

1 teaspoon (5 mL) kosher salt

½ teaspoon (2 mL) red chili flakes

2 sprigs fresh thyme

2 bay leaves

1 cup (250 mL) dry white wine

1 cup (250 mL) heavy (35%) cream

ROAST VENISON RACK

One 8-bone rack of venison (1½ to 2 pounds/675 g to 900 g)

Kosher salt and black pepper

2 to 3 tablespoons (30 to 45 mL) Spice Ash

2 tablespoons (30 mL) grapeseed oil or vegetable oil, for searing

A tagine is one of my favourite ways to cook a tougher cut of meat that is often overlooked and even thrown away by hunters. A tagine has two meanings. First, it refers to the cone-shaped cooking vessel that is typically made of ceramic or clay. Second, it refers to the stew-like dish that is braised in the vessel. Shanks are one of the most flavourful cuts because of the bone and the delicious marrow inside them. Lamb shanks can be substituted, but the cooking time will be shorter, as they are smaller. The spiced chutney nicely complements the game flavour of venison.

There are a few variables to consider when braising: the age of the animal, whether it was wild or farmed, and the consistency of your oven. Braising can sometimes take 3 hours or more, so be patient.

VENISON SHANK TAGINE WITH APRICOT CHUTNEY

Serves 4 to 6

Make the Apricot Chutney

In a medium saucepan, combine the apricots, sugar, white wine vinegar, shallots, garlic, mustard seeds, chili flakes and salt. Simmer over low heat, stirring frequently, until all the liquid has been absorbed, 15 to 20 minutes. The apricots should look plump and the chutney should have the consistency of thick jam. Remove from the heat. *(The chutney can be made ahead and stored in a sealed jar in the fridge for up to 2 weeks.)*

Cook the Venison Shank Tagine

Preheat the oven to 335°F (170°C).

Season the venison shanks with salt and pepper. Heat a large cast-iron or other heavy pot over high heat. Add the grapeseed oil to the pan. Using tongs, place the shanks in the hot pan and cook, without moving, for 3 to 4 minutes or until golden brown on the bottom. Turn and cook for another 3 to 4 minutes, without moving, to achieve a golden brown crust. Transfer the shanks to a plate.

Reduce the heat to medium and add the onion, carrot, and celery. Cook, stirring occasionally, until the vegetables begin to soften, 4 to 5 minutes. Add the cilantro, ginger, garlic, thyme, coriander seeds, cinnamon sticks, and bay leaves; stir to combine, then cook for 2 minutes. Put the shanks and any juices back in the pot and add the stock, tomatoes and their juice, saffron threads and liquid, and lemon zest and juice. Bring to a low

APRICOT CHUTNEY

1 cup (250 mL) dried apricots, roughly chopped
1 cup (250 mL) granulated sugar
1 cup (250 mL) white wine vinegar
¼ cup (60 mL) minced shallot
1 teaspoon (5 mL) minced garlic
1 teaspoon (5 mL) mustard seeds
½ teaspoon (2 mL) red chili flakes
¼ teaspoon (1 mL) kosher salt

VENISON SHANK TAGINE

4 pounds (1.8 kg) venison shanks (about 4 shanks)
Kosher salt and black pepper
2 tablespoons (30 mL) grapeseed oil or vegetable oil, for frying
2 cups (500 mL) diced Spanish onion (1 large onion)

recipe and ingredients continues

simmer. Cover the pot, transfer to the oven, and braise the shanks for 1½ hours before checking the meat. It is ready when it can be easily pulled from the bone but is not falling apart. If it is not ready, continue cooking, checking every 30 minutes. Discard the cinnamon sticks and bay leaves before serving.

Serve the tagine over couscous or rice, with a dollop of apricot chutney on top.

———————

Tip If you can, braise the meat the day before you plan to serve it. I find braised dishes taste better the next day.

1 cup (250 mL) diced carrot

1 cup (250 mL) diced celery

½ cup (125 mL) chopped fresh cilantro

¼ cup (60 mL) grated fresh ginger

2 tablespoons (30 mL) minced garlic

1 tablespoon (15 mL) chopped fresh thyme

2 teaspoons (10 mL) coriander seeds

3 cinnamon sticks

4 bay leaves

4 cups (1 L) Venison Stock (page 70) or beef stock

2 cans (28 ounces/796 mL each) diced tomatoes

1 teaspoon (5 mL) saffron threads, soaked in 2 tablespoons (30 mL) warm water

Zest and juice of 2 lemons

Cooked couscous or rice, for serving

This is a classic chili recipe, but I use venison instead of beef. Any red game meat or blend of game meats can be used instead of venison. Chili is a perfect way to use up the trimmed meat from the butchering process. I love the meat that's trimmed from between the ribs because its higher fat content gives it a rich flavour.

Omit the cayenne pepper if you do not like heat or have children who are sensitive to spice.

VENISON CHILI

Serves 6 to 8

2 tablespoons (30 mL) grapeseed oil or vegetable oil, for sautéing

1½ pounds (675 g) ground venison

2 cups (500 mL) diced Roma tomatoes (about 6 tomatoes)

1 cup (250 mL) diced white onion

½ cup (125 mL) diced celery

2 tablespoons (30 mL) minced garlic

3 tablespoons (45 mL) chili powder

1 tablespoon (15 mL) ground cumin

½ teaspoon (2 mL) cayenne pepper

½ teaspoon (2 mL) red chili flakes

2 teaspoons (10 mL) kosher salt

1 teaspoon (5 mL) freshly ground black pepper

2 cups (500 mL) Venison Stock (page 70) or beef stock

1 can (28 ounces/796 mL) crushed tomatoes

1 can (19 ounces/540 mL) kidney beans, drained and rinsed

3 tablespoons (45 mL) tomato paste

TOPPINGS

½ cup (125 mL) full-fat sour cream

½ cup (125 mL) grated smoked cheddar cheese

½ cup (125 mL) sliced green onions (white and light green parts only)

½ cup (125 mL) chopped fresh cilantro

¼ cup (60 mL) minced jalapeño pepper

In a large pot over high heat, heat the grapeseed oil. Add the ground venison, breaking it apart with a wooden spoon, and let the meat brown for 3 to 4 minutes before stirring.

Add the tomatoes, onion, celery, and garlic and sauté for 5 minutes. Add the chili powder, cumin, cayenne, chili flakes, salt, and black pepper. Stir to incorporate, then add the venison stock, crushed tomatoes, kidney beans, and tomato paste. Reduce the heat to medium-low and simmer, uncovered and stirring every 10 to 15 minutes, until thickened to your liking, 45 to 60 minutes.

Ladle the chili into warmed bowls and garnish with desired toppings.

Bolognese is a classic Italian meat ragù traditionally served with tagliatelle, a broad flat egg noodle. This is a hearty family meal. Making fresh pasta dough is a fun activity to involve your kids in. My kids love to get their hands into the dough and see their labour turn into rich noodles. You can use store-bought fresh or dried pasta if you do not have time to make your own. In place of the ground venison, you could use moose, elk, or any red meat of your choice.

VENISON BOLOGNESE WITH TAGLIATELLE

Serves 6

Venison Bolognese

Heat a large, heavy pot over high heat. Add the olive oil, ground venison, salt, and pepper and cook, stirring with a wooden spoon, until the meat is browned. Add the onion, carrot, celery, garlic, and chili flakes and cook, stirring occasionally, for 2 minutes. Add the stock, white wine, tomatoes and their juice, tomato paste, bay leaves, and thyme. Reduce the heat to medium-low and simmer, uncovered, until the sauce has thickened, 45 to 60 minutes. (Meanwhile, make the pasta dough.) Remove from the heat, discard the bay leaves and thyme stems, and keep warm while you cook the pasta.

Make the Tagliatelle

In the bowl of a stand mixer fitted with the dough hook, combine the egg yolks, bread flour, salt, and olive oil. Mix on low speed until a stiff dough forms, 3 to 5 minutes. The dough should stick together and feel like dry, stiff play dough when squeezed into a ball with your hand. If the dough appears sandy and it is not coming together to form a ball, add up to 1 tablespoon (15 mL) of water and continue mixing for 1 minute more. (Egg yolks vary in size, so a bit of water will help to form the dough. But be careful—too much water will soften the dough, resulting in a flimsy texture when cooked.)

Lightly flour a work surface with bread flour. Transfer the dough to the work surface and knead by hand to form a tight ball. Cover with plastic wrap and let rest for 30 minutes to relax the gluten before rolling and cutting. The dough can be wrapped in plastic wrap and stored for up to 12 hours or overnight in the fridge. Do not store the dough longer than 12 hours or it will start to oxidize, becoming yellowish grey.

VENISON BOLOGNESE

2 tablespoons (30 mL) olive oil, for sautéing

1 pound (450 g) ground venison

1 tablespoon (15 mL) kosher salt

2 teaspoons (10 mL) black pepper

1 cup (250 mL) diced white onion

½ cup (125 mL) diced carrot

½ cup (125 mL) diced celery

¼ cup (60 mL) minced garlic

Pinch of red chili flakes

2 cups (500 mL) dark stock (venison, game, or beef; see page 70)

1 cup (250 mL) dry white wine

1 can (28 ounces/796 mL) diced tomatoes

2 tablespoons (30 mL) tomato paste

3 bay leaves

2 sprigs fresh thyme

recipe and ingredients continues

Cut the dough into 2 equal portions. Press 1 portion flat with your hands and dust it with bread flour to prevent sticking. (Keep the remaining dough covered with plastic wrap.) Starting with the widest setting on a pasta machine, roll the dough twice through each setting until you've reached the first or second thinnest setting (about ⅟₁₆ inch/2 mm thick), dusting with bread flour as needed (do not over-flour). Cut the pasta into tagliatelle noodles, ¼ inch (5 mm) wide and 12 inches (30 cm) long, and portion into 4.25-ounce/120 g nests and dust with semolina flour to prevent sticking. *(If not using right away, freeze in an airtight container for up to 1 week. After that the pasta will become brittle and crack. Do not thaw before cooking.)*

Cook the Pasta and Finish

In a large pot of boiling salted water, cook the pasta until al dente, 2 to 3 minutes. The pasta will continue to cook when tossed in the sauce, so do not overcook it. Drain the pasta, return it to the pot, and toss with 2 ladlefuls of sauce, the butter, basil, and Parmesan. Serve in warmed bowls with more sauce and Parmesan on top, as desired.

Tip For best results with the pasta, use a digital scale and prepare the dough the day before and freeze in an airtight container.

TAGLIATELLE

10 extra-large egg yolks (preferably organic or omega-3 eggs for colour)
3 cups (750 mL/360 g) unbleached bread flour, more for dusting
1 teaspoon (5 mL) kosher salt
1 tablespoon (15 mL) olive oil
Semolina flour, for dusting

TO FINISH

2 tablespoons (30 mL) unsalted butter
4 sprigs fresh basil, leaves only
½ cup (125 mL) freshly grated Parmesan cheese, more for serving

Wild boars were brought to Canada from Europe and Asia as part of an agricultural diversification program. The idea was to commercialize the hogs as exotic meat. The animals are incredibly smart and strong, and some inevitably escaped and bred in the wild. As well, the market for the meat was not as lucrative as hoped, so some were released into the wild with the expectation that they would not survive the harsh Canadian climate. Well, they did survive the weather, and quite well. Their numbers are booming in the western provinces, where they are causing quite a lot of agricultural damage.

Boar meat is considerably darker in colour than pork. The wild pigs are generally less fatty than farm-raised boars, and their meat has a naturally gamey flavour from their more diverse omnivorous diet in the wild. Farm-raised wild boar is readily available in butcher shops and some grocery stores. Pork can easily be used in its place, but its flavour is subtler.

The pasta recipe requires a hand-cranked cavatelli machine or a wooden gnocchi board; both are available at kitchen stores and online. Fresh or frozen store-bought cavatelli pasta can be substituted.

WILD BOAR CAVATELLI

Serves 4 to 6

Make the Wild Boar Ragout
Preheat the oven to 325°F (160°C).

Heat a deep, heavy skillet or medium pot over high heat. Add the grapeseed oil to the pan. Add the boar meat, season with salt, peppercorns, and freshly ground pepper to taste, then reduce the heat to medium. Let the meat fry for 2 minutes without stirring. Then stir the meat, add the onion and celery, and cook for another 2 minutes. Add the garlic, juniper, and chili flakes and cook for another 2 minutes. Add the stock, white wine, bay leaves, and tomatoes. Cover with a lid or foil, transfer to the oven, and braise for 1 to 1½ hours. (Meanwhile, make the pasta.) Check the meat by pressing it with a fork. It should break apart. If it is not fork-tender, continue cooking, checking every 30 minutes. Discard the bay leaves. Keep the ragout warm while you cook the pasta. *(The ragout can be made ahead. Cool to room temperature and store in the fridge for up to 1 week.)*

WILD BOAR RAGOUT

2 tablespoons (30 mL) grapeseed oil or vegetable oil, for sautéing

1½ pounds (675 g) wild boar or pork shoulder, cut into ¾-inch (2 cm) cubes

2 teaspoons (10 mL) kosher salt

1 teaspoon (5 mL) black peppercorns

Freshly ground black pepper

1 cup (250 mL) diced white onion

½ cup (125 mL) diced celery

2 tablespoons (30 mL) minced garlic

2 tablespoons (30 mL) freshly ground juniper berries

recipe and ingredients continues

Make the Cavatelli

In the bowl of a stand mixer fitted with the dough hook, combine the bread flour, ½ cup (125 mL) of the semolina flour, egg, ricotta cheese, milk, salt, pepper, and nutmeg. Mix on low speed for 5 minutes. The dough should come together to look and feel like soft, pliable play dough. If not, add 1 tablespoon (15 mL) of water at a time and continue mixing. Cavatelli is more like a dumpling and the dough is not tight and firm. Let the dough rest, covered, at room temperature for 30 minutes.

On a lightly floured work surface, roll out the dough into a ½-inch (1 cm) thick sheet. Cut the dough into ½-inch (1 cm) wide strips. Feed the strips one at a time through the cavatelli machine. Dust the cavatelli with the remaining ¼ cup (60 mL) semolina flour and toss gently to prevent them from sticking together. (If you do not have a cavatelli machine, cut the strips into ½-inch × ¼-inch/1 cm × 5 mm rectangles. Using a wooden grooved gnocchi board, roll each piece of dough down the board, pressing and pushing with your thumb until the dough curls around itself and rolls off the board.) Use the fresh pasta within an hour. (*The cavatelli can be made ahead. Spread them on a baking sheet lined with parchment paper to prevent them from sticking together and freeze. Transfer to resealable plastic bags and freeze for up to 1 month. Do not thaw before cooking.*)

Cook the Pasta and Finish

In a large pot of boiling salted water, cook the cavatelli until they float, about 1 minute. Drain and add to the ragout. Add the Parmesan, butter, and basil. Toss or stir to incorporate and ladle into warmed bowls.

1 teaspoon (5 mL) red chili flakes
2 cups (500 mL) homemade light duck, game, or chicken stock (see page 70)
1 cup (250 mL) dry white wine
4 bay leaves
1 can (28 ounces/796 mL) crushed tomatoes

CAVATELLI

2½ cups (625 mL/300 g) unbleached bread flour
½ cup (125 mL) + ¼ cup (60 mL) semolina flour, divided
1 large egg
1 cup (250 mL) ricotta cheese
¼ cup (60 mL) whole milk
1 teaspoon (5 mL) kosher salt
Pinch of freshly ground black pepper
Pinch of freshly grated nutmeg
2 tablespoons (30 mL) cold water, as needed

TO FINISH

1 cup (250 mL) freshly grated Parmesan cheese
½ cup (125 mL) unsalted butter
1 bunch fresh basil, leaves only, chopped

Curing and smoking your own bacon is easy and incredibly rewarding. Pork belly can be substituted, but it's usually much bigger than the belly of a wild boar and takes a few more days to cure and more time in the smoker. If you are using meat with the skin on, it can be removed quite easily after cooking.

Carbonara is a classic pasta dish hailing from Rome and consisting of bacon, hard cheese, and eggs. Pecorino Romano or Parmesan cheese can be used, as well as any variety of pasta. Traditionally carbonara is finished with an egg cracked into the pan and tossed to incorporate into the sauce. Instead, I crack a duck egg yolk on top. The rich yolk deliciously oozes into the sauce.

CARBONARA WITH WILD BOAR BACON AND DUCK EGG YOLK

Serves 4

Make the Wild Boar Bacon

Place the boar belly in a large airtight container. In a small bowl mix together the salt, brown sugar, peppercorns, juniper, garlic, bay leaves, and thyme. Evenly cover the boar belly with the salt mixture. Cover the container with a lid and store in the fridge for 1 week. (Alternatively, using a vacuum sealer will cut the curing time in half.)

Remove the boar belly from the container, discarding the salt mixture. Rinse off the excess salt mixture under cold running water and dry with paper towel. In the smoker, smoke the belly, fat side up on a baking sheet, at 235°F (110°C) for 2 to 3 hours or until the internal temperature has reached 165°F (74°C). Cool the bacon in the fridge. (Slicing the bacon is much easier when it is chilled.) Transfer the bacon to an airtight container and store in the fridge for up to 1 week. Save any pan drippings to use in pastry or cooking.

Make the Carbonara

In a large, heavy skillet over medium heat, render the diced wild boar bacon and cook until it begins to crisp and turn golden, 3 to 5 minutes. Remove from the heat.

In a large pot of boiling salted water, cook the pasta until it floats, 30 to 60 seconds. Drain the pasta, reserving ¼ cup (60 mL) of the cooking water. Return the skillet with the bacon to medium heat and add the pasta, cubed butter, reserved cooking water, ¼ cup (60 mL) of the

WILD BOAR BACON

4 pounds (1.8 kg) wild boar belly or pork belly

2 cups (500 mL) kosher salt (I use Diamond Crystal)

1 cup (250 mL) packed brown sugar

2 tablespoons (30 mL) black peppercorns

1 tablespoon (15 mL) cracked fresh juniper berries

4 cloves garlic, crushed

4 bay leaves

1 bunch fresh thyme

CARBONARA

7 ounces (200 g) Wild Boar Bacon, diced

4 nests (about 17 ounces/480 g total) fresh tagliatelle (page 81) or store-bought

½ cup (125 mL) unsalted butter,

recipe and ingredients continues

cheese, salt, chili flakes, and black pepper. Toss or stir to combine, creating a sauce in the pan.

Portion the pasta into warmed bowls. Make a small well in the middle of the pasta and carefully place a duck egg yolk in the well. Garnish with the remaining ¼ cup (60 mL) cheese, the chives, black pepper to taste, and flaky sea salt.

———————

Tip If you do not have a smoker, you can roast the boar belly in the oven at the same temperature and cooking time.

cut into cubes
½ cup (125 mL) freshly grated
    Pecorino Romano or
    Parmesan cheese, divided
½ teaspoon (2 mL) kosher salt
Pinch of red chili flakes
2 teaspoons (10 mL) freshly
    ground black pepper
4 duck egg yolks
2 tablespoons (30 mL) chopped
    fresh chives
Flaky sea salt, for garnish

Homemade lasagna is my all-time favourite comfort food. The rich, creamy, crispy cheesy bits around the edges are heaven in a casserole dish.

Fresh pasta sheets are by far superior to dried ones and are easy to make. They do not need to be blanched in boiling water first and can be rolled out and cut to the exact size of your casserole dish. I use moose in this filling, but you could use any game or meat of your choice.

MOOSE LASAGNA

Serves 8

Make the Moose Meat Filling

Heat a large, heavy pot over high heat. Add the olive oil, butter, and ground moose, stir with a wooden spoon, and cook until the meat is brown, 5 to 6 minutes. Add the onion, carrot, celery, garlic, salt, black pepper, and chili flakes. Cook, stirring occasionally, for 2 minutes. Add the stock, diced tomatoes and their juice, tomato paste, bay leaves, and thyme. Reduce the heat to medium-low and simmer, uncovered and stirring occasionally, until the sauce has thickened, about 45 minutes. You do not want to reduce the liquid too much, as the fresh pasta sheets will cook in the moisture from the filling. Discard the bay leaves and thyme stems. Reserve 2 cups (500 mL) of the meat sauce.

Make the Ricotta Filling

In a medium bowl, using a whisk or wooden spoon, mix together the eggs, ricotta cheese, Parmesan, salt, and pepper until blended and smooth.

Make the Pasta

In the bowl of a stand mixer fitted with the dough hook, combine the flour, salt, whole eggs, egg yolks, and olive oil. Mix on low speed until a stiff dough forms, 3 to 5 minutes. The dough should stick together and feel like dry, stiff play dough when squeezed into a ball with your hand. If the dough appears sandy and is not coming together to form a ball, add up to 1 tablespoon (15 mL) of water and continue mixing for 1 minute more. (Egg yolks vary in size, so a bit of water will help to form the dough. But be careful—too much water will soften the dough, resulting in a flimsy texture when cooked.)

MOOSE MEAT FILLING

2 tablespoons (30 mL) olive oil

2 tablespoons (30 mL) unsalted butter

1 pound (450 g) ground moose

1 cup (250 mL) diced white onion

½ cup (125 mL) diced carrot

½ cup (125 mL) diced celery

¼ cup (60 mL) minced garlic

1 tablespoon (15 mL) kosher salt

2 teaspoons (10 mL) black pepper

Pinch of red chili flakes

2 cups (500 mL) homemade dark stock (venison, game, or beef; see page 70)

1 can (28 ounces/796 mL) diced tomatoes

2 tablespoons (30 mL) tomato paste

3 bay leaves

2 sprigs fresh thyme

recipe and ingredients continues

Transfer the dough to a lightly floured work surface and knead by hand to form a tight ball. Cover with plastic wrap and let rest for 30 minutes to relax the gluten before rolling and cutting. The dough can be wrapped in plastic wrap and stored for up to 12 hours or overnight in the fridge. Do not store the dough longer than 12 hours or it will start to oxidize, becoming yellowish grey.

Using a pasta machine, roll the dough down to the first or second thinnest size ($\frac{1}{16}$ inch/2 mm thick). This is done by starting at the thickest setting on the machine, then working down to the thinner setting. Dust the dough with flour before feeding it into the machine to avoid sticking. Cut 6 sheets of pasta to fit a 9- × 13-inch (3.5 L) baking dish (or to fit your lasagna pan).

Assemble and Bake the Lasagna

Preheat the oven to 350°F (180°C).

Spread a ladleful of the meat sauce over the bottom of the baking dish. Top with a sheet of pasta. Evenly spread one-third of the ricotta filling over the pasta and top with fresh basil leaves. Lay another sheet of pasta on top. Spread another ladleful of meat sauce over the pasta and top with a quarter of the grated mozzarella. Alternate layering meat sauce and mozzarella, pasta, and ricotta filling and basil until the casserole dish is full, about 6 layers of pasta. (You may not use all the pasta.) Finish with a layer of the meat sauce topped with the remaining grated mozzarella. Sprinkle the Parmesan over the top. If possible reserve some sauce for serving.

Cover with plastic wrap, then foil, and bake for about an hour. Test the doneness with a wooden skewer. It is done when it is hot throughout and there is no resistance from undercooked pasta. Remove the foil and plastic wrap and bake for an additional 15 to 20 minutes, until the cheese is golden and develops a crust. The broiler can be used for 3 to 5 minutes as well. Let the lasagna sit for 5 to 10 minutes before slicing.

Serve with the reserved moose meat sauce on top and a sprinkle of grated Parmesan and fresh basil leaves.

RICOTTA FILLING

2 eggs

3 cups (750 mL) ricotta cheese

1 cup (250 mL) freshly grated Parmesan cheese

1 teaspoon (5 mL) kosher salt

½ teaspoon (2 mL) freshly ground black pepper

PASTA DOUGH

3¾ cups (925 mL/450 g) all-purpose flour, more for dusting

1 teaspoon (5 mL) kosher salt

3 whole eggs (125 g)

6 egg yolks (115 g)

2 tablespoons (30 mL) olive oil

TO ASSEMBLE

2 bunches fresh basil, leaves only

1 ball (7 ounces/200 g) mozzarella cheese, coarsely grated

½ cup (125 mL) freshly grated Parmesan cheese, more for serving

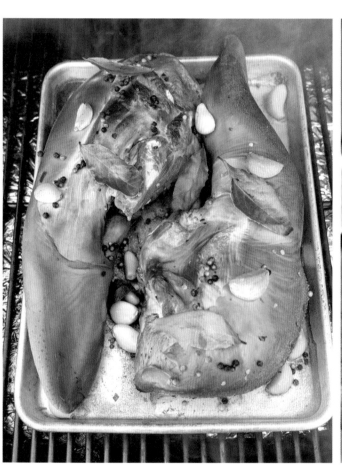

Moose tongue is similar in size and flavour to beef tongue. If you are a lover of Old World cuisine, this one is for you. I can guarantee that most of your hunting buddies don't want the tongues and will happily give theirs to you—until you make them this sandwich. Pastrami is made by brining the meat in water with salt and spices and then hot-smoking until tender.

MOOSE TONGUE PASTRAMI REUBEN SANDWICHES

Makes 5 to 6 sandwiches

Make the Brine

In a medium pot over high heat, bring the water, salt, peppercorns, coriander seeds, thyme, bay leaves, and curing salt to a boil. Remove from the heat and let cool to room temperature. (Alternatively, boil half the amount of water and add the rest of the water cold from the tap to speed up the cooling.) Submerge the moose tongue in the cooled brine and weight it down with a small plate or pot lid. Cover and store in the fridge for 5 days. The texture of the tongue will be firm to the touch when brined.

Smoke the Moose Tongue

Set the smoker to 225°F (110°C) and smoke the tongue for 2½ to 3 hours. (If you do not have a smoker, you can cook the moose tongue on a baking sheet in an oven at the same temperature for the same length of time.) The meat should easily pull from itself when cooked. Remove from the smoker and cover with foil or plastic wrap while hot. (This will make peeling the tongue easier.) When the tongue is cool enough to handle, using your fingers, peel off the skin. Cool the tongue in the fridge. Thinly slice to serve.

Assemble and Cook the Sandwiches

Heat a cast iron griddle or large skillet over medium heat.

In small bowl, stir together the ketchup and mayonnaise to make a Russian dressing. For each sandwich, spread the dressing on 2 slices of bread. Top one slice with sauerkraut, sliced tongue, and Swiss cheese. Top with the second slice of bread. Butter both outsides of the sandwich. Grill the sandwich for 3 to 5 minutes per side, until golden brown and the cheese has melted. Repeat to make the remaining sandwiches. Serve with sliced dill pickles and additional dressing for dipping.

1 moose tongue (3 to 4 pounds/1.35 to 1.8 kg)

BRINE

12 cups (3 L) water
¾ cup (175 mL) kosher salt (I use Diamond Crystal)
½ cup (125 mL) black peppercorns
½ cup (125 mL) coriander seeds
½ bunch fresh thyme
4 bay leaves
1 teaspoon (5 mL) curing salt (Prague Powder #1)

FOR THE SANDWICHES

½ cup (125 mL) ketchup
½ cup (125 mL) mayonnaise or aioli
1 loaf caraway rye bread, sliced
2 cups (500 mL) sauerkraut, drained and patted dry
10 to 12 slices Swiss cheese or cave-aged Emmental cheese
½ pound (225 g/1 cup/250 mL) unsalted butter, at room temperature, for grilling
Sliced dill pickles, for garnish

SMALL GAME

MY FIRST HUNT

MY FIRST HUNT SPOILED ME for life. Twice.

It was early spring of 2004, just before dawn on the edge of a farmer's field near Caledon, Ontario. The hunters had built a simple blind, a pile of fallen trees in the corner where the plough furrows met the woods. The guys had placed two decoys in the field. Decoys that could only fool a birdbrain. It was the start of turkey season.

They started with the calls. It's a sharp sound, like a crow's caw. It meant nothing to my eighteen-year-old ears. But to a turkey it's a military bugle, an assembly call. Then we waited for the turkeys to come.

The first hard lesson about hunting is, it should not be called *hunting*. It should be called *waiting*. And I do not mean waiting like a layover in an airport. You are in a group but you cannot talk. You cannot move. One cough can blow your cover for the day. There is no sign announcing the arrival of Air Turkey. And no matter how long you wait, you can always wait longer. And we did. Finally, one of the guys left the blind and went for a walk with his turkey call. He returned after a few minutes. "I saw a tom." We kept waiting. Sitting there for all that time in all that quiet, you start to feel a connection with our prehistoric ancestors. Patience, vigilance—and then action.

Nine of them came in amongst the stubble: six hens, two jakes, and then the tom. The jake is an adolescent male. They have these tiny beards. The tom has a giant beard that swings from side to side. The turkeys' gobbles echoed in the cold morning air. The hair on the back of my neck was standing. In the fifteen years since that morning, I have never seen so many birds on a hunt. The hunters had two tags, so they took two birds: the tom and a jake.

The kill is just one step in the process from hunter to chef. I quickly learned that the feathers pull more easily when the body is still warm.

At eighteen, I had already been cooking for five years. I knew my stuff. However, I had never stopped to consider the turkey as an animal rather than poultry. When I was growing up, the feast turkey was all about the breast meat, big and plump. As I butchered our birds, it was obvious to me that the wild turkey is a completely different animal. Wild turkey breast is flatter. The skin is yellow, the meat much darker.

When I tucked into my share, my first impression was, "This is not turkey." A fellow hunter said, "That's because you've never had turkey before. The shit you buy at the supermarket isn't turkey." It's like growing up with generic table syrup and then tasting real maple syrup for the first time. That was a light-bulb moment for me. *This is how turkey is supposed to taste.* I decided immediately that I did not want to eat factory-raised meat anymore. Spoiled for life, again.

Morel mushrooms and wild leeks (ramps) grow in hardwood forests in the spring and pair beautifully. Wild leeks take a very long time to grow, about seven years from a seedling to when the plant can produce its own seed, then take two years to germinate. When foraging for leeks, pick no more than 5 percent of a patch and try to rotate your picking spots year to year. If you can't find morels, feel free to use your favourite mushrooms from your grocery store or local market. You can stuff single breasts (as here) or the cavity of a whole bird.

ROASTED WILD TURKEY WITH GOAT CHEESE, MOREL MUSHROOM, AND WILD LEEK STUFFING

Serves 4 to 6

Stuff and Cook the Turkey

Preheat the oven to 350°F (180°C).

In a large saucepan over medium heat, melt 1 cup (250 mL) of the butter. Add the onion, celery, morels, chopped leek bulbs, and garlic. Cook, stirring occasionally, until soft, 3 to 4 minutes. Add the goat cheese, leek greens, and cubed bread and stir to combine. Remove from the heat and let cool to room temperature before stuffing the turkey breasts.

Using a boning knife, make a 2-inch (5 cm) cut along the fat end of each turkey breast and push the knife into the centre, making a pocket along the inside of the entire breast. Gently fill the breasts with the stuffing.

Heat a large skillet over medium heat. Add the olive oil and the remaining 1 tablespoon (15 mL) butter. Season the turkey breasts all over with salt and pepper and gently sear both sides. Transfer to the oven and cook to an internal temperature of 165°F (74°C), 20 to 30 minutes. Let the meat rest for 5 to 10 minutes before slicing.

STUFFED WILD TURKEY

1 cup (250 mL) + 1 tablespoon (15 mL) unsalted butter, divided

½ cup (125 mL) minced white onion

¼ cup (60 mL) minced celery

½ pound (225 g) morel mushrooms, washed, patted dry, and chopped

½ pound (225 g) wild leeks, white bulbs separated from green leaves and chopped

4 teaspoons (20 mL) minced garlic

1 pound (450 g) soft goat cheese, crumbled

3 cups (750 mL) cubed white sourdough or artisanal bread, crusts removed

2 boneless wild turkey breasts (about 1 pound/450 g each)

1 tablespoon (15 mL) olive oil

1 teaspoon (5 mL) kosher salt

Freshly ground black pepper

recipe and ingredients continues

Cook the Wild Spring Vegetables

While the turkey rests, in a large skillet over medium heat, melt the butter with the olive oil. Add the morels, fiddleheads, asparagus, and peas. Season with a pinch each of salt and pepper and cook until the vegetables are tender, 3 to 4 minutes, shaking the pan occasionally to toss the vegetables so they cook evenly. Remove from the heat.

To serve, slice the turkey breasts and divide among plates along with the vegetables. Garnish with pickled wild leeks.

WILD SPRING VEGETABLES

1 teaspoon (5 mL) unsalted butter

1 teaspoon (5 mL) olive oil

¼ pound (115 g) morel mushrooms, washed, patted dry, and cut in half lengthwise

¼ pound (115 g) fiddleheads, washed and drained

1 pound (450 g) asparagus spears, trimmed

1 cup (250 mL) freshly shucked green peas

Kosher salt and pepper

Pickled Wild Leeks (page 230), for garnish

This dish is a fun way to feature fowl offal on a plate. I love the flavour and richness of the heart, liver, and gizzard. I came up with this recipe when I found watercress while hunting for wild turkeys one morning along the riverbank. Goose, chicken, or duck offal can be used instead.

When making the port jus, be sure to use homemade stock. Store-bought stock does not thicken when reduced.

PAN-ROASTED TURKEY HEARTS AND LIVERS WITH CONFIT GIZZARDS, WATERCRESS CREAM, AND MORELS

Serves 4

Make the Confit Gizzards

In a container, combine the gizzards and salt, cover, and store in the fridge overnight.

Preheat the oven to 225°F (110°C).

Remove the gizzards from the container. Rinse off the salt with water and pat dry. Put the gizzards in a small oven-safe saucepan and pour in the duck fat. Slowly heat the duck fat and gizzards over low heat until warmed. Do not bring to a boil. Transfer to the oven and cook until tender, 2½ to 3 hours. Keep warm until ready to serve. *(The confit gizzards can be made ahead and stored, in the duck fat, in an airtight container in the fridge for up to 3 months.)*

Make the Port Jus

In a medium saucepan, combine the dark stock, port, shallot, thyme, bay leaf, and peppercorns. Boil over high heat until thick and reduced to about ½ cup (125 mL), 20 to 30 minutes. Strain and keep warm. *(The jus can be made ahead and stored in an airtight container in the fridge for up to 1 week.)*

Make the Watercress Cream

In a medium saucepan over medium heat, gently cook the watercress with the salt until wilted, 1 to 2 minutes. Add the cream and bring to a boil. Purée the mixture in a blender. Strain the cream back into the pan and keep warm. Discard the solids.

CONFIT GIZZARDS

4 turkey gizzards (14 ounces to 1 pound/400 to 450 g total)
½ cup (125 mL) kosher salt, for curing
2 cups (500 mL) duck fat, melted

PORT JUS

4 cups (1 L) homemade dark turkey or game stock (see page 70)
1 cup (250 mL) ruby port
1 shallot, minced
2 sprigs fresh thyme
1 bay leaf
1 tablespoon (15 mL) black peppercorns

WATERCRESS CREAM

2 cups (500 mL) chopped fresh watercress
Pinch of kosher salt
1 cup (250 mL) heavy (35%) cream

recipe and ingredients continues

Pan-Roast the Turkey Hearts, Livers, and Morels

Season the turkey hearts and livers with salt and pepper. Heat a medium cast-iron skillet over medium-high heat. Add the oil and butter. Add the hearts and livers and sear for 1 minute per side. The livers and hearts should be medium-rare doneness. (If you are using chicken offal, cook until the internal temperature is 165°F/74°C.) Remove the hearts and livers from the pan. Add the morels and sauté until tender, about 2 minutes.

To serve, slice the confit gizzards and turkey hearts and livers and arrange on plates with the morels, caramelized onions, port jus, and watercress cream. Garnish with fresh garlic mustard leaves and flowers.

PAN-ROASTED TURKEY HEARTS, LIVERS, AND MORELS

4 turkey hearts (about 6 ounces/170 g total)

4 turkey livers (about 8 ounces/225 g total), any large veins removed

Kosher salt and black pepper

1 tablespoon (15 mL) each grapeseed oil or vegetable oil and unsalted butter, for frying

½ pound (225 g) morel mushrooms, washed, patted dry, and cut in half

TO SERVE

¼ cup (60 mL) Caramelized Onions (page 65)

Fresh garlic mustard leaves and flowers, for garnish

One of the best leftover foods is a half-eaten roast turkey. My favourite way to use the leftover bird is to make stock with the bones and pot pie with the meat and that stock. Flaky, buttery pastry on top of a rich turkey stew is a classic comfort dish.

WILD TURKEY POT PIE

Makes 1 pie, serves 6 to 8

Preheat the oven to 375°F (190°C).

In a large saucepan, melt the butter over medium heat. Add the mushrooms, onion, carrot, celery, garlic, thyme, and rosemary and stir to combine. Cook, stirring occasionally, until the onions are soft and translucent, 3 to 4 minutes. Sprinkle the flour overtop and stir to make a paste. Cook for 1 minute more. Slowly add the milk while quickly stirring to prevent lumps. Add the turkey stock, shredded turkey meat, peas, salt, pepper to taste, and chili flakes. Stir to combine, then remove from the heat.

On a lightly floured work surface, roll out the quick puff pastry dough to a 10-inch (25 cm) circle.

Spoon the turkey mixture into a 9-inch (23 cm) pie plate. Top with the pastry round and trim the edge to about ½ inch (1 cm) over the rim. Fold the top edge under the bottom edge and seal by pressing firmly with your thumb against the rim of the pie plate. Brush the top of the pastry with egg wash. Bake until the pastry is a deep golden brown, 1 to 1½ hours.

1 batch of Quick Puff Pastry Dough (page 224)
⅓ cup (75 mL) unsalted butter
½ cup (125 mL) chopped mushrooms (I like morels, but you can use oyster or shiitake)
⅓ cup (75 mL) diced white onion
⅓ cup (75 mL) diced carrot
⅓ cup (75 mL) diced celery
2 teaspoons (10 mL) minced garlic
2 teaspoons (10 mL) chopped fresh thyme
1 teaspoon (5 mL) chopped fresh rosemary
⅓ cup (75 mL) all-purpose flour
1 cup (250 mL) whole milk
1 cup (250 mL) homemade wild turkey or chicken stock (see page 70)
2 cups (500 mL) shredded cooked turkey meat
⅓ cup (75 mL) fresh green peas
1 teaspoon (5 mL) kosher salt
Freshly cracked black pepper
Pinch of red chili flakes
1 egg yolk, lightly beaten, for egg wash

The ruffed grouse is a non-migratory game bird found from the Appalachian Mountains all the way to Alaska. It is smaller than a chicken, though it's often called a bush chicken. It has a delicious white/pinkish meat very similar to partridge and pheasant. If you cannot find ruffed grouse, good alternatives are partridge, pheasant, or spruce grouse (slightly darker meat). If using spruce grouse, be careful not to overcook it or it releases an irony spruce flavour.

Black walnuts are native to Canada and fun to forage. Resembling a lime in colour and shape, they are easy to spot on the ground in the fall. The nuts inside resemble walnuts in shape and flavour, with a hint of apple medicinal taste. Wear gloves when opening the walnuts, as the liquid in the skin will stain your hands black for several weeks. I know from experience! The sumac brings a lemony flavour to the dish without the acid changing the texture of the meat like lemon juice would.

SUMAC-MARINATED RUFFED GROUSE WITH BLACK WALNUT STUFFING

Serves 4 as an appetizer, 2 as a main

SUMAC-MARINATED RUFFED GROUSE

2 deboned ruffed grouse (about 8 ounces/225 g each), cut in half lengthwise (see Butchery Guide, page 22)

½ cup (125 mL) sumac berries

½ bunch fresh thyme

4 cloves garlic, crushed

Pinch of freshly ground black pepper

2 tablespoons (30 mL) olive oil

1 tablespoon (15 mL) unsalted butter, for searing

BLACK WALNUT STUFFING

½ cup (125 mL) unsalted butter

½ cup (125 mL) minced shallot

¼ cup (60 mL) minced celery

2 tablespoons (30 mL) minced garlic

2 tablespoons (30 mL) chopped fresh thyme

2 cups (500 mL) whole grain bread, crusts removed and cut into small cubes

½ pound (225 g) black walnuts, chopped

½ cup (125 mL) peeled and grated apple

1 teaspoon (5 mL) kosher salt

Pinch of freshly cracked black pepper

Prepare the Ruffed Grouse

Place the grouse halves in a large container and cover with the sumac berries, thyme, garlic, pepper, and olive oil. Cover and marinate overnight in the fridge.

Make the Black Walnut Stuffing

Heat a medium saucepan over medium heat. Add the butter, shallots, celery, garlic, and thyme and cook, stirring occasionally, until the shallots and celery are soft, 2 to 3 minutes. Add the cubed bread, walnuts, apple, salt, and pepper. Stir to combine. Remove from the heat and let cool to room temperature before stuffing the birds.

Stuff and Cook the Ruffed Grouse

Preheat the oven to 350°F (180°C).

Wipe the marinade off the meat using paper towel and discard the marinade. Mound a handful of the stuffing in the middle of the inside of each breast. Fold the leg over to close and tie shut with butcher twine.

In a medium skillet over medium-high heat, melt the butter. Sear the grouse, starting skin side down, until the skin is golden brown. Transfer to the oven and cook for 5 to 6 minutes. Ruffed grouse does not have the same bacteria as farm-raised chicken and I prefer it a little pink, with an internal temperature of about 145°F (63°C). If you are nervous about eating wild game, cook to 165°F (74°C) to kill any bacteria. Let rest for 3 minutes before slicing into 1-inch (2.5 cm) pieces.

Ruffed grouse remind me of my childhood. I remember the thudding sound of their drumming wings—like a lawn mower trying to start—during their mating season. During the fall, when we are roaming the logging roads looking for moose or bear to hunt, we often spot grouse swallowing gravel to ingest into their gizzard to aid digestion. Unfortunately for them, their defence instinct is to freeze, making them easy targets. When they are in the forest and fields their camouflage is immaculate, and dogs are used to flush them up into the air to give them more of a sporting chance.

No matter how you choose to hunt them, their meat is delicious. Here is a very simple way to cook them whole over a campfire during hunting season. You can cook grouse in the oven, of course, but it is much more fun outside. This dish is a fun play on fried chicken and waffles. The grouse skin is roasted crispy and the pancakes are a fun and easy substitution to make at the hunt camp.

FIRE-ROASTED RUFFED GROUSE

Serves 4

Brush the grouse with 1 tablespoon (15 mL) of the grapeseed oil and season with salt and pepper. Hang the grouse with twine or wire 3 to 4 feet (1 to 1.2 m) over a campfire and slowly cook until the internal temperature reaches 135°F (57°C) for medium doneness or up to 165°F (74°C) for well done. (Alternatively, you can sear the birds in a large cast-iron skillet with 1 tablespoon/15 mL of the grapeseed oil and roast in a 275°F/140°C oven for 45 to 60 minutes.)

While the birds are slowly roasting, in a small saucepan, combine 1 tablespoon (15 mL) of the grapeseed oil, apples, and cinnamon, Cook over medium heat for 3 minutes. Add the sugar and cook until the apples are soft, stirring occasionally, 10 to 15 minutes. Remove from the heat and keep warm.

When the birds are cooked to your liking, fry the pancakes using the remaining grapeseed oil as needed. Serve the grouse with the pancakes and apple sauce, with maple syrup, if desired.

4 whole ruffed grouse (about 1 pound/450 g each)
½ cup (125 mL) grapeseed oil or vegetable oil, divided
1 teaspoon (5 mL) kosher salt
Freshly cracked black pepper
2 crisp tart green apples (such as Granny Smith, Gala, or Honeycrisp), peeled and diced
1 batch of Wild Blueberry Pancake batter, without the blueberries (page 220)
1 teaspoon (5 mL) cinnamon
½ cup (125 mL) granulated sugar
Pure maple syrup, for serving (optional)

Waterfowl are any aquatic game bird. The waterfowl meat for this dish is prepared by confiting, or slowly cooking the meat in duck fat. This method is great for tougher legs like those of ducks or geese. The silky rich foie gras adds a creamy texture to the terrine.

Prepare this dish at least 1 day before you plan to serve it, to allow it to set. Thinly sliced, it is an impressive appetizer or addition to a charcuterie board.

WATERFOWL AND FOIE GRAS TERRINE

Makes 1 terrine

Cure the Waterfowl and Foie Gras

In a small bowl, mix together 1 cup (250 mL) of the kosher salt, ½ teaspoon (2 mL) of the curing salt, sugar, garlic, cinnamon, star anise, coriander, and bay leaves. Place the waterfowl legs in a large airtight container and cover with the salt mixture. Cover the container and cure in the fridge for 3 days. The meat will be firm in texture from the curing.

On the second day of curing, combine the foie gras and the milk in a large container, cover, and refrigerate for 24 hours. Remove the foie gras, rinse under cold running water, and pat dry with paper towel. Let the foie gras come to room temperature. Using a paring knife or toothpick, gently remove any large veins you can see at the end of the lobe. Cut the foie gras into 1-inch (2.5 cm) pieces and place in a large airtight container. In a small bowl, mix together ½ cup (125 mL) of the kosher salt and mixed with the remaining ½ teaspoon (2 mL) curing salt; then evenly sprinkle over the foie gras. Cover the container and let the foie cure in the fridge overnight or up to 12 hours.

Preheat the oven to 300°F (150°C).

Rinse the waterfowl legs under cold running water and pat dry with paper towel. In a large, heavy pot over medium heat, melt 1 tablespoon (15 mL) of the solid duck fat and sear the legs, skin side down, until golden, 3 to 4 minutes. Turn over and cook for an additional 1 minutes. Add the remaining solid duck fat and heat until warm throughout. Transfer to the oven and cook until the meat can be easily pulled from the bone, 2½ to 3 hours.

1½ cups (375 mL) + 1 teaspoon (5 mL) kosher salt, divided (I use Diamond Crystal)

1 teaspoon (5 mL) curing salt (Prague Powder #1), divided

¾ cup (175 mL) granulated sugar

2 teaspoons (10 mL) minced garlic

1 teaspoon (5 mL) cinnamon

½ teaspoon (2 mL) ground star anise

½ teaspoon (2 mL) ground coriander

2 bay leaves

5 pounds (2.25 kg) waterfowl legs (such as snow goose, duck, Canada goose)

½-pound (225 g) piece foie gras

2 cups (500 mL) whole milk

8 cups (2 L) solid duck fat

1 cup (250 mL) melted duck fat

3 tablespoons (45 mL) minced shallot

1 tablespoon (15 mL) chopped fresh thyme

2 tablespoons (30 mL) red wine vinegar

½ teaspoon (2 mL) black pepper

recipe continues

Assemble the Terrine

Line a 9- × 6-inch (23 × 15 cm) terrine mould with plastic wrap, leaving some wrap overhanging the long sides to cover the terrine. Cut a piece of cardboard or wood to fit just inside the mould.

Remove the legs from the duck fat and let cool slightly. Pull all the meat from the bones and discard the bones. Save the used duck fat and store in the fridge in an airtight container to use in other recipes and cooking.

In a large bowl, combine the pulled duck meat, foie gras, minced shallot, thyme, red wine vinegar, the remaining 1 teaspoon (5 mL) salt, pepper, and melted duck fat. Mix until well combined. Firmly push all of the meat mixture into the terrine, making sure there are no air pockets. Fold the overhanging plastic wrap over the top to cover. Place the piece of heavy cardboard or wood over the terrine and weigh it down with a heavy can or jar. Allow the terrine to set in the fridge for 24 hours before slicing. Store tightly wrapped in plastic wrap in the fridge for up to 2 weeks or in the freezer for up to 6 months.

This dish was inspired by a friend's dad at duck camp one fall. We came back to camp after a successful hunt and had a meal of freshly harvested duck breast with eggs and a side of baked beans mixed with raisins and cut-up hotdogs. It may sound pedestrian to you but it's an amazing meal to come home to when you have been freezing out on the marsh.

In this recipe I've replaced the hotdogs with duck legs, but sometimes I'll use a spicy chorizo sausage and serve it over these smoked cheddar grits with braised kale.

ROAST DUCK WITH MAPLE BAKED BEANS AND GRITS

Serves 4 to 6

Make the Grits

In a medium pot, combine the grits and water. Cover with a lid and soak overnight at room temperature.

Bring the grits and water to a boil over high heat. Cover with a lid, reduce the heat to low, and simmer, stirring frequently with a wooden spatula to prevent sticking and burning, for 2 to 3 hours. (Alternatively, you can use a slow cooker, but the grits will take longer to cook.) When the grits are soft and have the texture and appearance of porridge, stir in the smoked cheddar, butter, and salt. Remove from the heat and keep warm.

Meanwhile, Make the Maple Baked Beans

Preheat the oven to 350°F (180°C).

Season the duck legs with salt and pepper. Heat a large pot over high heat. Add the grapeseed oil, then sear the duck legs on both sides, working in batches if necessary. Add the tomatoes, water, kidney beans, maple syrup, molasses, raisins (if using), chili flakes, paprika, oregano, allspice, bay leaves, thyme, salt, and pepper. Bring to a simmer. Cover with a lid, transfer to the oven, and bake until the beans and the duck legs are tender, 2½ to 3 hours.

Remove the duck legs from the beans and pull the meat from the bones. Discard the bones. Return the duck meat to the pot and, if needed, simmer the beans over medium-low heat to thicken. Season to taste with salt and pepper. Discard the bay leaves and thyme stems. Keep warm.

GRITS

2 cups (500 mL) grits

8 cups (2 L) water

½ cup (125 mL) grated smoked cheddar cheese

2 tablespoons (30 mL) unsalted butter

1 tablespoon (15 mL) kosher salt

MAPLE BAKED BEANS

6 mallard duck legs (about 6 ounces/170 g each; use 8 to 10 legs if smaller)

1 tablespoon (15 mL) grapeseed oil or vegetable oil, for frying

1 can (28 ounces/796 mL) crushed tomatoes

6 cups (1.5 L) water

3 cups (750 mL) dried kidney beans (soaked overnight in water and drained)

1½ cups (375 mL) pure maple syrup

½ cup (125 mL) fancy molasses

1 cup (250 mL) raisins (optional)

recipe and ingredients continues

Roast the Duck Breasts

Score the skin of the duck breasts with a sharp knife, making long, shallow incisions first lengthwise, then horizontally. Be careful not to cut into the meat. This will allow the fat to escape and result in a crispier skin. Season both sides of the breasts with the salt and pepper.

Heat 2 large cast-iron skillets (or cook in batches in one pan) over medium heat. Place the duck breasts in the pan skin side down. The heat will render the fat out of the skin. Gently cook the duck until the skin caramelizes to a golden brown and is crispy to the touch, 3 to 5 minutes. If you notice the meat curl, you can place a pan on top of the duck to gently press down. Turn the breasts and cook for 1 minute. Remove from the pan and let rest for 3 to 5 minutes.

Thinly slice the duck breasts against the grain and serve with the maple baked beans and grits.

1 tablespoon (15 mL) red chili flakes

1½ teaspoons (7 mL) smoked paprika

1½ teaspoons (7 mL) dried oregano

1 teaspoon (5 mL) ground allspice

2 bay leaves

4 sprigs fresh thyme

1 tablespoon (15 mL) kosher salt, more for seasoning

1 teaspoon (5 mL) black pepper, more for seasoning

ROAST DUCK BREASTS

6 boneless duck breasts (4 to 6 ounces/115 to 170 g each)

1 tablespoon (15 mL) kosher salt

1 teaspoon (5 mL) freshly ground black pepper

Roasting a duck crown—the double breast on the bone without the wings and legs—is a great way to cook a duck. Meat tastes better when cooked on the bone. The breasts will take a bit longer to heat through but the skin slowly roasts and the fat renders, giving the duck more time to get crispy. I had a teacher in chef school tell us that nobody likes a soggy duck, and he was right!

DUCK CROWN ROAST

Serves 4

Preheat the oven to 325°F (160°C).

Season the duck with the salt and pepper. Heat a large skillet over medium heat. Sear the duck, skin side down, with the rosemary and garlic until light golden, 2 to 3 minutes, per side. Transfer to the oven and roast the duck for 30 to 45 minutes, until the internal temperature reaches 125°F (50°C) for medium-rare doneness (red centre). If the skin is not as crispy as you would like, place under the broiler for 2 to 3 minutes, but be careful not to burn the skin. Let rest for 6 to 8 minutes before slicing.

2 duck crowns (2 pounds/900 g each)
1 tablespoon (15 mL) kosher salt
1 teaspoon (5 mL) freshly cracked black pepper
4 sprigs fresh rosemary
4 cloves garlic, crushed

Confit hails from France and it is an age-old method of preservation. Traditionally duck, goose, or pork is salt-cured with herbs, then gently cooked in its own fat, and then cooled and stored in its own fat keeping it airtight. Moist and succulent, confit meat can be shredded cold to add to salads or reheated to crisp the skin and served as a main course. Confit is a great staple to have on hand, and an excellent to use duck and goose legs from your hunts.

You can find duck fat in specialty butcher shops or render your own from a collection of your own harvests.

DUCK CONFIT

Serves 8

In a medium bowl, stir together the salt, sugar, juniper berries, thyme, bay leaves, and garlic. Place the duck legs in a large casserole dish and cover with the salt mixture. Cover and cure in the fridge for 2 or 3 days.

Preheat the oven 300°F (150°C).

Rinse the duck legs under cold running water and pat dry with paper towel. In a large, heavy pot over medium heat, melt 1 tablespoon (15 mL) of the duck fat. Sear the legs, starting skin side down, until golden all over. Add the remaining duck fat and heat until warm throughout. Cover with a lid or foil, transfer to the oven and cook until the meat can be easily pulled from the bone, 2½ to 3 hours.

If storing the confit, make sure there is enough fat to cover the meat to protect it from air; store in the fridge for up to 6 months, always keeping the meat covered with fat. Alternatively, the duck confit can be sealed in glass jars following proper canning procedures and stored in a cold cellar.

1 cup (250 mL) kosher salt (I use Diamond Crystal)

½ cup (125 mL) granulated sugar

2 tablespoons (30 mL) juniper berries

½ bunch fresh thyme

4 bay leaves

8 cloves garlic

8 duck or goose legs (about 8 ounces/225 g each)

12 cups (3 L) duck fat, divided

A liver parfait is much creamier and softer in texture than a traditional pâté. This recipe is rich in flavour and silky smooth. Slice the parfait with a wet knife (use hot water) or spread on sliced bread and serve with Wild Blueberry Compote (page 219) or other sweet compote or jam. You can use chicken livers in place of the duck livers.

DUCK LIVER PARFAIT

Makes 1 terrine

Put the duck livers in a medium container with a lid and cover with the milk. Cover and let soak overnight in the fridge.

In a small saucepan, combine the port, shallots, thyme, bay leaf, and peppercorns. Bring to a boil over high heat and reduce the liquid until almost all of it has evaporated, 5 to 10 minutes. Add the brandy and simmer to boil off the alcohol, 1 to 2 minutes. Remove from the heat and discard the thyme stems and bay leaf. Set aside.

Preheat the oven to 350°F (180°C). Line a 9- × 6-inch (23 × 15 cm) terrine mould with plastic wrap.

Drain the duck livers and discard the milk. Rinse the livers under cold running water and pat dry with paper towel.

In a small saucepan, bring the cream to a simmer, then remove from the heat. In a blender, combine the egg yolks, duck fat, butter, reserved shallot mixture, duck livers, kosher salt, and curing salt. While blending, very slowly pour in the hot cream, blending until smooth. Pour the mixture through a fine-mesh sieve to remove any veins from the livers and large bits of shallot.

Pour the strained mixture into the prepared terrine mould and cover with the mould's lid or foil. Place the terrine in a small roasting pan or casserole dish with high sides. Place the pan in the oven, then carefully add boiling water to the pan until it comes halfway up the sides of the terrine mould. Bake until the terrine is set but still slightly jiggly, 30 to 45 minutes. Carefully remove the terrine from the water bath and let cool to room temperature. When cool, transfer to the fridge to set overnight.

Invert the terrine onto a cutting board and slice it, or spoon it into a piping bag, pipe into small jars, cover with melted butter or duck fat to seal, and store in the fridge for up to 2 weeks.

¾ pound (340 g) duck livers, any veins removed

2 cups (500 mL) whole milk

1 cup (250 mL) ruby port

½ cup (125 mL) sliced shallot

4 sprigs fresh thyme

1 bay leaf

1 tablespoon (15 mL) black peppercorns

2 tablespoons (30 mL) brandy

1 cup (250 mL) heavy (35%) cream

2 egg yolks

½ cup (125 mL) duck fat, at room temperature

½ cup (125 mL) unsalted butter, at room temperature

2 teaspoons (10 mL) kosher salt

1 teaspoon (5 mL) curing salt (Prague Powder #1)

This smoked duck breast is best enjoyed cold as an appetizer or on a charcuterie board. It is delicious served with mustard or a sweet-and-sour garnish. The rich gamey flavour of duck is enhanced by the smoky flavour.

If you do not have a smoker, you can place 2 cups (500 mL) of wood chips in foil and place the pouch directly on one side of a barbecue burner over low heat.

CURED SMOKED DUCK BREASTS

Serves 4 to 6

In a small bowl, stir together the salt, sugar, and allspice. Place the rosemary in a casserole dish and sprinkle half of the salt mixture over the rosemary. Place the duck breasts skin side up on top of the salt. Sprinkle the rest of the salt mixture over the duck breasts to cover. Cover and cure in the fridge for 3 days.

Rinse the duck breasts under cold running water and pat dry with paper towel. Set the smoker to 265°F (130°C) and smoke the duck until the internal temperature reaches 140°F (60°C), about 2 hours. Chill, then store tightly wrapped in plastic wrap in the fridge for up to 1 month. Thinly slice to serve.

½ cup (125 mL) kosher salt (I use Diamond Crystal)

¼ cup (60 mL) granulated sugar

1 tablespoon (15 mL) whole allspice, cracked

2 sprigs fresh rosemary

2 pounds (900 g) boneless duck breast (4 breasts)

Duck hearts are small, but put a few on a skewer and you have a beautiful snack. Best served rare to medium, these duck hearts are brushed with a sweet soy glaze, a recipe given to us by my business partner and book photographer Jody's mother-in-law from Japan, where there are restaurants dedicated to yakitori (the word means grilled chicken that is cooked over a charcoal fire). In these yakitori bars all parts of the chicken are skewered and grilled. Heart, gizzard, liver, and skin are common types of yakitori.

Chicken hearts can be substituted, but they need to be cooked until well done.

DUCK HEART YAKITORI

Serves 4 as an appetizer

If you are using bamboo or wooden skewers, soak them in water overnight to prevent them from burning.

In a small saucepan, combine the soy sauce, mirin, sake, rice malt, sugar, orange juice, and lemon juice. Bring to a boil over high heat and cook until the liquid is reduced by a third, 5 to 10 minutes. Let cool to room temperature.

Skewer the duck hearts on bamboo skewers or cedar sticks, 3 or 4 to a skewer.

Prepare the grill for direct cooking over high heat for 10 minutes.

Brush the duck hearts with the cooled glaze and grill for 2 to 4 minutes per side, brushing a couple of times with more glaze while on the grill. The hearts should have nice char marks and be rare to medium doneness. Serve immediately.

1 cup (250 mL) soy sauce
½ cup (125 mL) mirin
¼ cup (60 mL) sake
¼ cup (60 mL) rice malt (koji)
¼ cup (60 mL) granulated sugar
Juice of 1 orange
Juice of 1 lemon
1 pound (450 g) duck hearts

This dish is a nod to my southern friends in Mississippi, where the food and the people have a lot of soul! I never really understood dove hunting until I tried it. They fight for the title of smallest game bird along with quail and woodcock, and I didn't see the point in shooting them. One day while I was hunting Canada goose, flocks of doves started flying in. Shooting at a bird so small and flying so fast was a real challenge!

Doves are a perfect size for a starter or snack, but for a main course you will need three or four per person. Quail can be substituted for dove.

FRIED DOVE WITH BUTTERMILK BISCUITS AND SAUSAGE GRAVY

Serves 4 to 6

FRIED DOVE

12 dove crowns (double breasts on the bone, wings and legs removed)

3 cups (750 mL) buttermilk

4 quarts (4 L) vegetable oil, for deep-frying

2 cups (500 mL) all-purpose flour

2 tablespoons (30 mL) smoked paprika

1 tablespoon (15 mL) garlic powder

1 teaspoon (5 mL) cayenne pepper

1 teaspoon (5 mL) kosher salt

1 teaspoon (5 mL) black pepper

BUTTERMILK BISCUITS

1¾ cups (425 mL/210 g) all-purpose flour

2½ teaspoons (12 mL) baking powder

½ teaspoon (2 mL) baking soda

⅓ cup (75 mL) cold unsalted butter

½ cup (125 mL) buttermilk

¼ cup (60 mL) heavy (35%) cream

1 egg

3½ teaspoons (17 mL) granulated sugar

1 teaspoon (5 mL) kosher salt

Soak the Dove

In a large container, cover the doves with the buttermilk. Cover and let soak in the fridge for at least 8 hours or overnight. This will help tenderize the meat.

Make the Buttermilk Biscuits

Preheat the oven to 425°F (220°C). Line a baking sheet with parchment paper.

In a food processor, combine the flour, baking powder, baking soda, and butter. Pulse until the mixture resembles pea-size crumbles. Add the buttermilk, cream, egg, sugar, and salt. Pulse until the dough just comes together. Do not overmix or the biscuits will be tough. Spoon the dough into 6 equal portions on the prepared baking sheet and bake until golden brown, 10 to 12 minutes. Set aside to cool.

recipe and ingredients continues

Make the Sausage Gravy

Break up the sausage meat in a medium skillet over medium-high heat and cook until brown, 2 to 3 minutes. Add the salt, then sprinkle the flour over the sausage to soak up the fat. Stir with a wooden spoon, making sure there are no lumps of flour. Stir in the milk, reduce the heat to low, and simmer until the gravy is thick, 3 to 4 minutes. Remove from the heat and keep warm.

Fry the Doves

In a large pot, heat the oil to 350°F (180°C) over medium-high heat.

In a large bowl, whisk together the flour, paprika, garlic powder, cayenne, salt, and black pepper. Remove the doves from the buttermilk, discarding the buttermilk, and dredge in the flour mixture. Fry until golden and floating, 3 to 5 minutes. Using tongs, remove the doves from the hot oil and drain on a rack or paper towel. Season with a pinch of salt.

To serve, arrange the biscuits on plates. Pour the sausage gravy over the biscuits and place the fried doves on top.

SAUSAGE GRAVY

½ pound (225 g) breakfast sausages, casings removed

½ teaspoon (2 mL) kosher salt

2 tablespoons (30 mL) all-purpose flour

2 cups (500 mL) whole milk

Many people believe that as a symbol of Canada, the Canada goose is protected from hunting and eating. In fact it can be hunted, and this majestic goose is actually considered a nuisance bird, with its population on the rise unaffected by urban sprawl and human interference. They are incredibly resilient birds, and in the wild their life expectancy can reach upward of twenty years. Keep in mind that a twenty-four-year-old wild gander won't be as tender as a younger farm-raised fowl, so proper care is required when preparing them in the kitchen. Canada goose breast meat is delicious when slow-roasted and served medium-rare, the legs are perfect for confit or braised dishes, and the large carcass is great for making stock.

In this recipe the goose is served two ways—roasted and braised. Cassoulet is a wonderfully rich and flavourful way to cook beans. Dry beans must be used as canned will become overcooked and mushy. Homemade stock is also the secret ingredient as store-bought stock does not have the same flavour and natural gelatin. The slow cooking process allows the beans to soak up all of the flavour of the stock and bacon, creating a beautiful, decadent flavour.

ROAST CANADA GOOSE BREAST AND CASSOULET

Serves 4 to 6

Place the kidney beans in a bowl, cover with water, and soak overnight at room temperature. The next day, drain well.

Preheat the oven to 350°F (180°C).

In a large pot, melt ¼ cup (60 mL) of the butter over medium heat. Add the boar bacon and cook for 3 minutes. Add the onion, carrot, celery, and garlic, stir to combine, and cook for another 2 minutes. Add the drained kidney beans, white wine, 4 cups (1 L) of the game stock, 1 teaspoons (5 mL) of the salt, 1 teaspoon (5 mL) of the pepper, thyme, bay leaves, and the confit goose legs. Bring to a simmer. Cover with a lid, transfer to the oven, and cook for 1½ to 2 hours, stirring occasionally and checking to see if the stock has all been absorbed, topping up with more stock as necessary. The beans should be plump and tender, with some liquid in the pot but it shouldn't be soupy. Discard the bay leaves and thyme stems before serving.

Reduce the oven temperature to 325°F (160°C).

Season the goose breasts with the remaining 1 teaspoon (5 mL) salt and 1 teaspoon (5 mL) pepper. In a large skillet, heat the grapeseed oil and the remaining 1 tablespoon (15 mL) butter over medium-high heat.

3 cups (750 mL) dried white kidney beans

¼ cup (60 mL) + 1 tablespoon (15 mL) unsalted butter, divided

½ pound (225 g) Wild Boar Bacon (page 87) or store-bought

1 cup (250 mL) diced onion

½ cup (125 mL) diced carrot

½ cup (125 mL) diced celery

6 cloves garlic

1 cup (250 mL) dry white wine

8 cups (2 L) light game or chicken stock, divided (see page 70)

2 teaspoons (10 mL) kosher salt, divided

2 teaspoons (10 mL) freshly cracked black pepper, divided

recipe and ingredients continues

Add the goose breasts skin side down and sear, turning once, until brown on both sides. Transfer to the oven and cook for 5 to 10 minutes, to an internal temperature of 125°F (50°C) for medium-rare or 135°F (57°C) for medium doneness. Let the meat rest for 5 to 8 minutes before serving.

Thinly slice the breast meat and serve on top of the cassoulet.

4 sprigs fresh thyme

2 bay leaves

4 confit goose legs (see Duck Confit, page 120, made with goose legs)

2 boneless Canada goose breasts (10 to 12 ounces/280 to 340 g each)

1 tablespoon (15 mL) grapeseed oil or vegetable oil, for searing

Sausages with mashed potatoes is a staple comfort food in England, and naturally I've worked wild game into the recipe. You can use any type of sausage you like, but here I have chosen Canada goose, which complements the sweetness of the onion and the earthy sage in the gravy. The trick to making great sausages is to use very cold meat by chilling the chopped meat in the freezer for 10 minutes before grinding. The grinder die, blade, and auger can also be chilled in the freezer with the meat. The friction of moving parts heats the meat and melts the fat, causing a grainy sausage if not properly chilled.

CANADA GOOSE BANGERS AND MASH WITH SAGE AND ONION GRAVY

Serves 4 to 6

Make the Goose Sausage

Soak the intestine in a large container of cold water for 30 minutes to release the curing salt they are packed in and soften the casing. Rinse under cold running water. If using synthetic casing, follow package directions.

Meanwhile, cut the goose and pork into 1-inch (2.5 cm) chunks. Spread the meat out on a baking sheet and freeze for 10 minutes. It is very important to chill the meat. When grinding meat, the friction of the grinder causes the meat to heat up. If it becomes too hot, the meat will oxidize faster and become grainy in texture.

Using a fine die, grind the meat through the grinder into a large bowl. Add the garlic, salt, fennel, chili flakes, and pepper. Mix using an electric mixer or by hand. If by hand, mix well. Mix by hand to incorporate. Add the meat to a sausage stuffer and press into the casings, making a large coil. Twist the sausage into 4- to 5-inch (10 to 12 cm) links and refrigerate until ready to cook. The fresh sausage will keep, vacuum-sealed or wrapped in butcher paper in an airtight container, in the fridge for up to 5 days or in the freezer for up to 6 months.

GOOSE SAUSAGE (MAKES 15 TO 20 SAUSAGES)

10 feet (3 m) pork intestine (or synthetic casing)

3 pounds (1.35 kg) Canada goose meat

2 pounds (900 g) fatty pork (shoulder, neck, or belly)

4 teaspoons (20 mL) crushed garlic

1 tablespoon (15 mL) kosher salt

1 tablespoon (15 mL) ground fennel

2 teaspoons (10 mL) red chili flakes

2 teaspoons (10 mL) black pepper

recipe and ingredients continues

Make the Sage and Onion Gravy

Preheat the oven to 400°F (200°C).

Wrap the whole skin-on onion with foil and roast on a small baking sheet until the onion is completely soft, mushy, and dark caramel in colour, 1 to 1½ hours.

Heat a medium saucepan over medium heat. (Alternatively, you can quickly make the gravy in the same pan the sausages are roasted in, using the pan drippings in place of butter.) Melt the butter in the pan, then add the flour, stir with a wooden spoon to make a paste, and cook, stirring, until the paste is golden. While whisking, add the game stock, ½ cup (125 mL) at a time, whisking constantly to prevent lumps. When all the stock has been added, pour in the white wine and simmer to thicken, 4 to 5 minutes. Remove from the heat.

Remove the onion from the foil. Cut away and discard the skin. Roughly chop the onion, then add the onion and sage to the gravy. Keep warm.

Make the Mashed Potatoes

In a large pot, cover the potatoes with cold water and add the salt. Simmer over medium heat until fork-tender, 10 to 15 minutes. Drain well. Mash the potatoes, then stir in the warm cream and melted butter. Stir in the grated cheese and nutmeg. Taste for seasoning and add a pinch of salt if needed. Keep warm.

Cook the Bangers

Preheat to the oven to 350°F (180°C).

Cook 6 of the sausages in a cast-iron skillet over medium heat for 2 to 3 minutes per side. Transfer to the oven and roast until the internal temperature reaches 165°F (74°C), 6 to 8 minutes.

To serve, spoon the mashed potatoes onto warmed plates. Top with the sausages and generously ladle the gravy on top.

SAGE AND ONION GRAVY

1 large Spanish onion, skin on
3 tablespoons (45 mL) unsalted butter
3 tablespoons (45 mL) all-purpose flour
2 cups (500 mL) homemade game stock or dark chicken stock (see page 70)
½ cup (125 mL) dry white wine
6 fresh sage leaves, roughly chopped

MASHED POTATOES

2 pounds (900 g) white potatoes, peeled
2 tablespoons (30 mL) kosher salt
1 cup (250 mL) heavy (35%) cream, warmed
1 cup (250 mL) unsalted butter, melted
1 cup (250 mL) grated white cheddar cheese
Pinch of freshly grated nutmeg

Foie gras is the ultimate delicacy, originally made in France but now also produced in Canada. The farming practices involved in making it have been controversial, but today farmers have adopted much more humane methods of producing the beautiful fatty liver.

When I teach cooks how to sear a slice of foie gras, I tell them to think of it as a slice of butter. It needs to be seared quickly, at a very high temperature, to crisp the outside, and it has to be removed from the heat instantly or it will simply melt away. The biscuit is a variation of the buttermilk biscuit on page 129, but instead of butter, the fat is, of course, foie gras. *(You'll need 1 lobe fresh foie gras. Use the end trimmings for the biscuits.)*

SEARED FOIE GRAS WITH FOIE GRAS BISCUITS AND PRESERVED CHERRIES

Serves 6 as an appetizer

Make the Preserved Cherries

In a medium saucepan, combine the brandy, sugar, and salt and boil over high heat for 2 to 3 minutes to cook off the alcohol. The brandy is flammable, so have a lid nearby in case the brandy ignites, and be careful not to spill any on the burner or let the pan boil over. Add the cherries and tarragon to the hot brandy and cook for 2 minutes. Remove from the heat and let cool to room temperature. *(The cherries can be made ahead and stored in an airtight container in the fridge for up to 1 month.)*

Make the Foie Gras Biscuits

Preheat the oven to 425°F (220°C). Line a baking sheet with parchment paper.

In a food processor, combine the foie gras, flour, baking powder, and baking soda. Blend just until the mixture has a crumble consistency. Do not purée it—you should see small lentil-sized bits of foie gras. Add the buttermilk, cream, sugar, salt, and egg. Pulse until the dough just comes together. Do not overmix or the biscuits will be tough. Spoon the dough into 6 equal portions on the prepared baking sheet and bake until golden brown, 10 to 12 minutes. Set aside to cool.

PRESERVED CHERRIES

1 cup (250 mL) brandy

1 cup (250 mL) granulated sugar

Pinch of kosher salt

1 pound (450 g) fresh sour cherries, pitted

3 sprigs fresh tarragon

FOIE GRAS BISCUITS

⅓ cup (75 mL/75 g) fresh foie gras (trimmings from lobe ends)

¾ cup (175 mL) all-purpose flour

2 teaspoons (10 mL) baking powder

½ teaspoon (2 mL) baking soda

½ cup (125 mL) buttermilk

¼ cup (60 mL) heavy (35%) cream

3½ teaspoons (17 mL) granulated sugar

1 teaspoon (5 mL) kosher salt

1 egg

recipe and ingredients continues

Make the Spiced Wine Glaze

In a medium saucepan, combine the red wine, sugar, cinnamon stick, star anise, juniper berries, and cloves. Bring to a boil over high heat and cook until the sauce is syrupy and has reduced to about 1 cup (250 mL).

Sear the Foie Gras

Heat a large cast-iron or other heavy skillet over high heat for 3 to 5 minutes. Make sure the kitchen exhaust fan is on high. Slice the foie gras horizontally across the lobe into 6 equal portions about ½ inch (1 cm) thick. Using a sharp knife, score one side of the foie gras slices in a crisscross pattern to allow the inner fat to reach the surface and the outside to crisp up. Season the foie gras on both sides with a pinch of salt. Working with 2 or 3 slices of foie gras at a time, place the foie gras, scored side down, in the pan with no additional oil. The foie gras will sizzle and smoke—this is normal. Do not move the foie gras. It will get a deep caramel crust in 30 to 60 seconds. Carefully turn and sear the other side for 5 to 10 seconds and immediately remove from the pan. The foie gras should be tender to the touch and just warm in the centre. If the middle feels hard, that means the fat in the centre is still cold and continue cooking for about 30 seconds.

Serve a slice of foie gras inside each foie gras biscuit, drizzled with the spiced wine glaze and with a spoonful of the preserved cherries on top and around the biscuits.

SPICED WINE GLAZE

2 cups (500 mL) dry red wine

1 cup (250 mL) granulated sugar

1 cinnamon stick

2 whole star anise

1 tablespoon (15 mL) juniper berries

1 tablespoon (15 mL) whole cloves

SEARED FOIE GRAS

1 pound (450 g) fresh foie gras lobe (frozen does not sear properly)

1 tablespoon (15 mL) kosher salt

Pigeon is in the same family as the mourning dove and its meat is very similar—dark in colour, rich in flavour like duck meat, and best eaten anywhere from rare to medium doneness. Pigeon is often referred to as squab in recipes, but technically a squab is a young pigeon that has not flown, therefore more tender. The sumac in the vinaigrette adds a tart lemony, earthy flavour to the salad that complements the dark meat of pigeon.

GRILLED PIGEON AND ARUGULA SALAD WITH SUMAC VINAIGRETTE

Serves 4

Make the Sumac Vinaigrette

In a small saucepan, bring the red wine vinegar and sumac berries to a simmer over medium heat. Remove from the heat once it starts to bubble. Let macerate for 4 hours at room temperature or overnight, covered, in the fridge. Strain the mixture into a medium bowl. Discard the sumac.

Whisk in the mustard, shallot, garlic, and salt. Slowly whisk in the olive oil and grapeseed oil until emulsified. (*The vinaigrette can be made ahead. Transfer to a glass jar, seal with a lid, and store in the fridge for up to 1 month. Shake to emulsify before using.*)

Make the Grilled Pigeon and Arugula Salad

Preheat a barbecue or grill to medium-high heat.

Season the pigeons with a pinch each of salt and pepper. Brush the grill with the grapeseed oil to prevent sticking. Grill the pigeons skin side down until the skin is crispy, 3 to 5 minutes. Turn the pigeons over and cook for 1 minute more.

In a large bowl, toss together the arugula, olives, tomatoes, cucumber, red onion, and 2 tablespoons (30 mL) of the sumac vinaigrette.

Divide the salad among plates and serve the pigeon on top.

SUMAC VINAIGRETTE

½ cup (125 mL) red wine vinegar
½ cup (125 mL) sumac berries
1 tablespoon (15 mL) Dijon mustard
1 tablespoon (15 mL) minced shallot
1½ teaspoons (7 mL) minced garlic
½ teaspoon (2 mL) kosher salt
½ cup (125 mL) olive oil
¾ cup (175 mL) grapeseed oil or vegetable oil

GRILLED PIGEON AND ARUGULA SALAD

2 pigeons (about 8 ounces/225 g each), cut in half
Kosher salt and black pepper
1 tablespoon (15 mL) grapeseed oil or vegetable oil, for grilling
8 ounces (225 g) baby arugula
1 cup (250 mL) Cerignola or other mild green olives, pitted
1 cup (250 mL) heirloom cherry tomatoes, cut in half
1 cup (250 mL) sliced English cucumber
½ cup (125 mL) thinly sliced red onion

The sweetness of the potato nicely balances the flavour of the pigeon and the richness of the flaky pastry. Because the legs and breasts of these birds are so small, you can make 6 or 8 individual pot pies instead of 1 large pie.

PIGEON AND SWEET POTATO POT PIE

Makes 1 pie, serves 6 to 8

Cut the backbone out of each pigeon. Separate the legs from the breasts, and remove and discard all the small bones. Season the pigeons with the salt and pepper. In a 9-inch (23 cm) cast-iron pan over high heat, heat the grapeseed oil. Working in batches if needed, sear the pigeon, skin side down, until golden, 3 to 5 minutes. Turn and cook the meat side for 1 to 2 minutes. Remove the pigeon.

Melt the butter in the pan over medium heat. Add the sweet potato, mushrooms, shallots, and garlic and cook, stirring occasionally, for 3 minutes. Sprinkle the flour overtop and stir to make a paste, then slowly add the milk while stirring to prevent lumps. Stir in the stock, thyme, allspice, and nutmeg. Return the pigeon to the sauce, remove from the heat, and pour the mixture into a 9-inch (23 cm) pie plate.

Preheat the oven to 375°F (190°C).

On a lightly floured work surface, roll out the butter pastry dough to a 10-inch (25 cm) circle to make a lid for the pie. Cut a vent hole in the centre of the pastry to allow the steam to escape. Brush the edges of the pastry with the egg wash and invert the pastry over the pan. Using your thumb, press the overhanging pastry against the side of the pan to seal. Brush the egg wash over the pastry. Bake until the pastry is golden brown, about 1 hour.

3 whole pigeons (about ¾ pound/340 g each)

1 teaspoon (5 mL) kosher salt

Pinch of freshly cracked black pepper

2 tablespoons (30 mL) grapeseed oil or vegetable oil, for searing

⅓ cup (75 mL) unsalted butter

1½ cups (375 mL) peeled and diced sweet potato

1 cup (250 mL) sliced oyster mushrooms

½ cup (125 mL) diced shallot

1 tablespoon (15 mL) minced garlic

¼ cup (60 mL) all-purpose flour

1 cup (250 mL) whole milk

1 cup (250 mL) homemade game, fowl, or chicken stock (see page 70)

2 teaspoons (10 mL) chopped fresh thyme

½ teaspoon (2 mL) ground allspice

Pinch of nutmeg

½ batch of Butter Pastry Dough (page 59)

1 egg yolk beaten with 1 tablespoon (15 mL) water, for egg wash

Lobster mushrooms are aptly named for their lobster taste and smell. The shellfish flavour of lobster mushrooms pairs beautifully with the gamey taste of pigeon. A surf-and-turf flavour without the shellfish.

PIGEON STUFFED WITH LOBSTER MUSHROOMS

Serves 6 as an appetizer

Preheat the oven to 350°F (180°C).

In a large saucepan, melt the butter over medium heat. Add the mushrooms and shallots and cook, stirring occasionally, for 3 minutes. Add the garlic, thyme, and diced bread and cook for another 2 or 3 minutes, stirring to combine. Let the mixture cool to room temperature before stuffing the pigeons.

Stuff the birds and tie with butcher twine. Season the birds with salt and pepper. Heat a large skillet over high heat. Add the grapeseed oil, then sear the pigeons on all sides to brown the skin. Transfer to the oven and roast for 15 to 25 minutes, until the internal temperature reaches 130°F (55°C). Let rest for 5 minutes. Slice each pigeon in half lengthwise and serve.

½ cup (125 mL) unsalted butter
1 pound (450 g) fresh lobster
    mushrooms, chopped
½ cup (125 mL) minced shallot
1 tablespoon (15 mL) minced
    garlic
1 teaspoon (5 mL) chopped fresh
    thyme
1 cup (250 mL) diced bread
3 whole pigeons (about
    12 ounces/340 g each)
Kosher salt and black pepper
1 tablespoon (15 mL) grapeseed
    oil or vegetable oil

I feel like pasta was made as a vessel for rabbit. Rich, buttery, cheesy noodles tossed with shredded rabbit meat and its braising liquid as the sauce is a beautiful combination. The acidity and sweetness in the preserved apricot provide the perfect balance to the rich egg pasta and cheese.

Verjus literally means "green juice." It is an unfermented juice pressed from the acidic low-sugar grapes that winemakers trim from the vines before they are ripe. It is less potent than vinegar and can be used in salad dressings or, as in this recipe, as a mild pickling liquid. Verjus is available in specialty grocery stores.

RABBIT PAPPARDELLE WITH BUTTER-BRAISED LEEKS AND PRESERVED APRICOT

Serves 5

Make the Preserved Apricot

Place the apricots in a resealable container or mason jar. In a small saucepan over high heat, combine the verjus, mustard seeds, and bay leaf. Bring to a boil over high heat and boil for 1 minute. Pour the hot verjus over the apricots. Let cool to room temperature, then seal the jar and let the apricots soak in the fridge for 24 hours before using. The preserved apricot will keep in the fridge for up to 1 month.

Make the Rabbit Braise

Preheat the oven to 325°F (160°C).

Heat a large pot over high heat. Season the rabbits all over with salt and pepper. Melt the butter with the oil in the pot, then sear the rabbits until golden on both sides, 2 to 4 minutes per side . Add the onion, celery, and garlic and cook, stirring occasionally, for 3 minutes. Add the game stock, white wine, thyme, and bay leaves. Cover with a lid or foil, transfer to the oven, and braise for about 1 hour. The meat should easily pull off the bone but not be falling apart to the touch.

Remove the rabbits from the braising liquid and let rest until cool enough to handle. Pull all the meat from the bones. Discard the bones. Add the meat back to the braising liquid.

PRESERVED APRICOT (MAKES EXTRA)

1 cup (250 mL) dried apricots

2 cups (500 mL) verjus

1 tablespoon (15 mL) mustard seeds

1 bay leaf

RABBIT BRAISE

4 pounds (1.8 kg) rabbit (2 whole rabbits)

1 tablespoon (15 mL) kosher salt

1 teaspoon (5 mL) black pepper

1 tablespoon (15 mL) each unsalted butter and grapeseed oil or vegetable oil, for sautéing

1 cup (250 mL) diced white onion

½ cup (125 mL) diced celery

4 cloves garlic

8 cups (2 L) homemade light game or chicken stock (see page 70)

2 cups (500 mL) dry white wine

½ bunch fresh thyme

4 bay leaves

recipe and ingredients continues

Meanwhile, Make the Butter-Braised Leeks

Melt the butter in a medium casserole dish. Cut the leeks in half length-wise, rinse and pat dry, then submerge in the butter. Add the salt. Cover and bake next to the rabbit for about 1 hour. The leeks should be soft and supple to the touch. Slice enough leeks to measure 1 cup (250 mL) and set aside.

Cook the Pasta and Finish the Dish

Bring a large pot of salted water to a boil over high heat.

In another large pot, combine the reserved pulled rabbit, 1 cup (250 mL) of the braising liquid, reserved sliced leeks, preserved apricots, butter, salt, pepper, and chili flakes. Stir over medium heat to heat through.

When the water is boiling, add the pappardelle and cook until the pasta floats, 2 to 3 minutes. When the pasta floats, cook for an additional 30 seconds. Strain the pasta and add to the pot with the rabbit mixture. Stir to combine. Add the Parmesan and stir again. Scoop into warmed bowls and serve.

BUTTER-BRAISED LEEKS

1 pound (450 g/2 cups/500 mL) unsalted butter

3 medium leeks, white and light green parts only), washed

1 teaspoon (5 mL) kosher salt

TO FINISH

⅓ cup (75 mL) sliced Preserved Apricot

½ cup (125 mL) unsalted butter

1 teaspoon (5 mL) kosher salt

Pinch of freshly cracked black pepper

Pinch of red chili flakes

1 batch ravioli dough (see page 149), rolled and cut into 1- × 12-inch ribbons (or 5 fresh pappardelle nests, 4.25 ounces/120 g each)

½ cup (125 mL) freshly grated Parmesan cheese

This stuffed pasta is a beautiful way to showcase rabbit meat. The rich pasta and subtle gamey rabbit, simply tossed with butter and basil and drizzled with aged balsamic vinegar, will be a favourite with your family and friends.

RABBIT RAVIOLI WITH BASIL AND AGED BALSAMIC

Serves 5

Make the Rabbit Filling

Preheat the oven to 325°F (160°C).

Heat a large pot over high heat. Season the rabbits all over with salt and pepper. Melt the butter with the oil in the pot, then sear the rabbits until golden on both sides, 5 to 10 minutes, total. Add the onion, celery, and garlic and cook, stirring occasionally, for 3 minutes. Add the game stock, white wine, thyme, bay leaves, and chili flakes. Cover with a lid or foil, transfer to the oven, and braise for about 1 hour. The meat should easily pull off the bone but not be falling apart to the touch.

Remove the rabbits from the braising liquid. Discard the bay leaves and thyme stems. Let the rabbits rest until cool enough to handle, then pull all the meat from the bones. Discard the bones. Return the meat to the braising liquid and simmer until the liquid is no longer watery and the rabbit meat is very tender. Cool the filling before stuffing the ravioli. The cooled mixture can be further broken up for easier stuffing of the ravioli.

Make the Ravioli

In the bowl of a stand mixer fitted with the dough hook, combine the egg yolks, bread flour, salt, and olive oil. Mix on low speed until a stiff dough forms, 3 to 5 minutes. The dough should stick together and feel like dry, stiff play dough when squeezed into a ball with your hand. If the dough appears sandy and is not coming together to form a ball, add up to 1 tablespoon (15 mL) of water and continue mixing for 1 minute more. (Egg yolks vary in size, so a bit of water will help to form the dough. But be careful—too much water will soften the dough, resulting in a flimsy texture when cooked.)

Lightly flour a work surface with bread flour. Transfer the dough to the

RABBIT FILLING

4 pounds (1.8 kg) rabbit
   (2 rabbits)
1 tablespoon (15 mL) kosher salt
1 teaspoon (5 mL) black pepper
1 tablespoon (15 mL) each
   unsalted butter and grapeseed
   oil or vegetable oil, for sautéing
1 cup (250 mL) diced white
   onion
½ cup (125 mL) diced celery
4 cloves garlic
8 cups (2 L) homemade light
   game or chicken stock (see
   page 70)
2 cups (500 mL) dry white wine
½ bunch fresh thyme
4 bay leaves
Pinch of red chili flakes

RAVIOLI DOUGH

10 extra-large egg yolks
   (preferably organic or
   omega-3 eggs for colour)
3 cups (750 mL/360 g)
   unbleached bread flour, more
   for dusting
1 teaspoon (5 mL) kosher salt
1 tablespoon (15 mL) olive oil

recipe or ingredients continues

work surface and knead by hand to form a tight ball. Cover with plastic wrap and let rest for 30 minutes to relax the gluten before rolling and cutting. The dough can be wrapped in plastic wrap and stored for up to 12 hours or overnight in the fridge. Do not store the dough longer than 12 hours or it will start to oxidize, becoming yellowish grey.

Press the dough flat with your hands and dust it with bread flour to prevent sticking. Starting with the widest setting on a pasta machine, roll the dough twice through each setting until you've reached the first or second thinnest size (about 1/16 inch/2 mm thick), making one long sheet. Fold the sheet in half lengthwise and press gently to form a crease. Open the dough up and cut along the crease. Cover one dough sheet with a plastic bag or damp cloth. Brush the other sheet with egg wash. Shape the rabbit filling into 45 to 50 balls (about 2 tablespoons/30 mL each) and place them about 1½ inches (4 cm) apart in a row down the centre of the pasta sheet. Cover with the other sheet of pasta and firmly but gently push down around each ball of filling with your fingers and the side of your hand to force out any air. Cut out ravioli using a square ravioli cutter or ravioli wheel. Sprinkle a baking sheet with semolina, arrange the ravioli on it, and sprinkle the ravioli with semolina to prevent sticking. Freeze for at least 1 hour before cooking.

Cook the ravioli in a large pot of boiling salted water until they float, 2 to 3 minutes. (If the ravioli have been frozen for more than 1 hour, boil for 4 to 5 minutes.) Drain the ravioli, reserving ¼ cup (60 mL) of the cooking water.

In a large bowl, toss the ravioli with the reserved cooking water, butter, basil, and Parmesan. Divide the pasta among plates, drizzle with aged balsamic vinegar, and serve.

1 egg yolk beaten with
1 tablespoon (15 mL) water, for egg wash
Semolina flour, for dusting

TO FINISH
½ cup (125 mL) unsalted butter
¼ cup (60 mL) chopped fresh basil
½ cup (125 mL) freshly grated Parmesan cheese
Aged balsamic vinegar, for drizzling

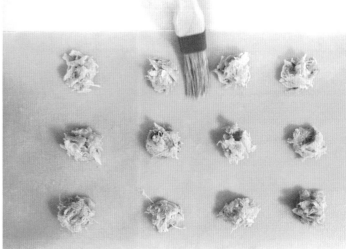

Squirrel is a sadly underrated game meat. You do not often hear your hunting buddies talking about their squirrel-hunting trips, favourite squirrel recipes, or squirrels they have managed to snap pictures of with their trail cameras. However, these little critters are in the same family as rabbit and are every bit as tasty. It tastes like chicken. The legs have the most meat and are seriously good grilled, stewed, or fried. Hunting squirrel is a great way to teach younger hunters how to hunt and clean their own wild game. Feel free to interchange poultry or fowl in any of the squirrel recipes.

SQUIRREL AU VIN

Serves 4

Preheat the oven to 350°F (180°C).

Chop each squirrel into 4 equal pieces and season with salt and pepper. Dredge in flour to coat well.

In a large, heavy pot over medium heat, melt the butter with the vegetable oil. Add the squirrel and bacon and cook until the squirrel is crispy and golden, turning to cook on all sides, 3 to 5 minutes total. Remove the squirrel from the pot. Add the mushrooms, pearl onions, celery, and garlic to the pot and cook, stirring occasionally, until the onions are translucent, 3 to 4 minutes. Deglaze with the red wine, brandy, and stock. Add the bay leaf, thyme, salt, pepper, and chili flakes. Return the squirrel to the pot, cover, and braise until the meat can be easily pulled from the bone and the back legs are tender, 1½ to 2 hours.

Remove the squirrel and set aside. Reduce the braising liquid over high heat until it is thick enough to coat the back of a spoon and add the squirrel back to the sauce. Taste for seasoning and add a pinch of salt if needed. Discard the bay leaf and thyme stems.

To serve, spoon into deep plates or bowls and garnish with chopped parsley and lemon zest.

4 squirrels (about 1 pound/450 g each)

¼ cup (60 mL) all-purpose flour, for dredging

1 tablespoon (15 mL) each unsalted butter and vegetable oil, for sautéing

½ cup (125 mL) diced bacon

1 cup (250 mL) chopped wild mushrooms (such as chanterelle, morel, oyster, or shiitake)

1 cup (250 mL) peeled pearl onions

½ cup (125 mL) diced celery

4 cloves garlic

1 cup (250 mL) dry red wine

¼ cup (60 mL) brandy

4 cups (1 L) homemade dark chicken or game stock (see page 70)

1 bay leaf

¼ bunch fresh thyme, chopped

2 teaspoons (10 mL) kosher salt, more for seasoning

1 teaspoon (5 mL) freshly ground black pepper, more for seasoning

Pinch of red chili flakes

2 tablespoons (30 mL) chopped flat-leaf parsley, for garnish

1 teaspoon (5 mL) lemon zest, for garnish

Squirrel is in the rabbit family, though to be honest, it tastes like chicken. This is my take on a classic barbecue dish but made with whole squirrels, served with fluffy, rich cornbread and sautéed green beans. For an added treat, spread soft butter over the cornbread and sprinkle with a pinch of sugar.

BARBECUED SQUIRREL WITH CORNBREAD

Serves 3 to 4

Marinate the Squirrel

In a small saucepan, combine the ketchup, maple syrup, red wine vinegar, Worcestershire sauce, brown sugar, paprika, and cayenne. Simmer over low heat until the sugar is dissolved and the barbecue sauce is well combined, 2 to 3 minutes. Let cool to room temperature. Put the squirrels in a container with a tight-fitting lid and pour the sauce over the squirrels to coat. Cover with the lid and marinate the squirrels in the fridge for at least 8 hours or overnight to tenderize the meat.

Make the Cornbread

Preheat the oven to 375°F (190°C). Grease a 9- × 5-inch (2 L) loaf pan.

In a large bowl, cream together the butter and sugar with an electric mixer on medium speed. Add the eggs, one at a time, beating well after each addition. Add the buttermilk and beat until combined. Add the cornmeal, flour, baking powder, baking soda, and salt and mix on low speed until the batter just comes together. Do not overmix. Scrape the batter into the prepared loaf pan and bake for 30 minutes or until a wooden skewer inserted in the middle comes out clean. Cool slightly before turning out of the pan and slicing.

Grill the Squirrel

Prepare the grill for direct cooking over medium-low heat.

Remove the squirrels from the marinade (reserving the marinade) and grill for 6 to 8 minutes per side until deep grill marks are visible, brushing occasionally with the marinade.

BARBECUED SQUIRREL

2 cups (500 mL) ketchup

½ cup (125 mL) pure maple syrup

¼ cup (60 mL) red wine vinegar

2 teaspoons (10 mL) Worcestershire sauce

¼ cup (60 mL) brown sugar

1 tablespoon (15 mL) smoked paprika

1 teaspoon (5 mL) cayenne pepper

4 squirrels (about 1 pound/450 g each)

CORNBREAD

¾ cup (175 mL) unsalted butter, more for serving

2 tablespoons (30 mL) granulated sugar

4 eggs

3 cups (750 mL) buttermilk

2 cups (500 mL) cornmeal

1½ cups (375 mL/180 g) all-purpose flour

3 tablespoons (45 mL) baking powder

1½ teaspoons (7 mL) baking soda

1 teaspoon (5 mL) kosher salt

¼ cup (60 mL) sliced green onion (white and light green parts only), for garnish

Sauté the Green Beans

Meanwhile, in a medium skillet over medium-high heat, sauté the green beans with the butter until crisp-tender, 2 to 3 minutes.

Serve the grilled squirrel with the green beans and warm cornbread topped with a dollop of butter, if desired, and garnished with sliced green onions.

SAUTÉED GREEN BEANS

12 ounces (340 g) green beans, trimmed

1 tablespoon (15 mL) unsalted butter

If you love fried chicken, you will love this recipe. The candied yams add a nice sweet touch to balance the salty, crispy fried squirrel. Yams or sweet potatoes can be used. I love an oil and vinegar dressing on coleslaw; the tart sumac vinaigrette cuts the richness of the fried squirrel.

FRIED SQUIRREL WITH CANDIED YAMS AND COLESLAW

Serves 3 to 4

Soak the Squirrel

Cut each squirrel into 4 equal pieces. In a large container, cover the squirrel with the buttermilk. Cover and let soak in the fridge for at least 8 hours or overnight to tenderize the meat.

Make the Candied Yams

Preheat the oven to 375°F (190°C). Line a baking sheet with parchment paper.

Cut the yams into ½-inch (1 cm) wedges. In a large bowl, toss the yams with the oil, brown sugar, and salt. Spread the yams on the prepared baking sheet and bake until caramelized and golden, with charred marks from the caramelizing sugar, 45 to 60 minutes.

Fry the Squirrel

In a large pot, heat the vegetable oil to 350°F (180°C) over medium-high heat.

In a large bowl, whisk together the flour, paprika, garlic powder, cayenne, salt, and black pepper. Remove the squirrel from the buttermilk, discarding the buttermilk, and dredge in the flour mixture. Fry until golden and floating, 6 to 8 minutes. Using tongs, remove the squirrel from the hot oil and drain on a rack or paper towel.

Serve the fried squirrel with ramekins of barbecue sauce, coleslaw, and candied yams.

FRIED SQUIRREL

4 squirrels (about 1 pound/450 g each)

3 cups (750 mL) buttermilk

8 cups (2 L) vegetable oil, for frying

2 cups (500 mL) all-purpose flour

2 tablespoons (30 mL) smoked paprika

1 tablespoon (15 mL) garlic powder

1 teaspoon (5 mL) cayenne pepper

1 teaspoon (5 mL) kosher salt

1 teaspoon (5 mL) black pepper

½ cup (125 mL) barbecue sauce (see page 154), for serving

CANDIED YAMS

3 large yams, peeled

2 tablespoons (30 mL) grapeseed oil or vegetable oil

2 tablespoons (30 mL) brown sugar

1 teaspoon (5 mL) kosher salt

Make the Coleslaw

In a large bowl, toss together the cabbage, onion, carrot, sumac vinaigrette, salt, and pepper.

COLESLAW

3 cups (750 mL) thinly sliced napa cabbage

1 cup (250 mL) thinly sliced red onion

1 cup (250 mL) peeled and shredded carrot

¾ cup (175 mL) Sumac Vinaigrette (page 141)

1 teaspoon (5 mL) kosher salt

½ teaspoon (2 mL) freshly ground black pepper

FISH AND FORAGE

MY FIRST CATCH

MY FIRST MEMORY OF FISHING was as a young child in the pond in the backyard of our home in the countryside. It was a bass pond, but there were sometimes trout, too. I used to play and swim for hours, catch frogs, overturn rocks and find crayfish. I once saw a frog swallowed in one gulp by a huge bass. That truly was a real-life lesson of the food chain. I learned how to fly-fish and tie flies from a family friend, and we would catch fish and eat them for dinner. I loved that pond.

Today I still love to fish. During the summer months, when most hunting seasons are closed, I enjoy fishing for pickerel, bass, trout, and the occasional pike. I have had many trips out with our commercial fishing friends on the west coast and the Great Lakes. I've also learned how to trap spot prawns and crabs. Recently I learned how to down-rig for salmon in Lake Ontario, where I was totally surprised that we had twenty- to thirty-five-pound fish living so close to the city. Fishing is a wonderful time to spend alone or with family and friends. For some reason my kids are a good-luck charm and always catch bigger fish than I do, but that's okay because we all get to enjoy eating them!

THE GREAT MOREL
MUSHROOM

FORAGING IS A WONDERFUL EXCUSE to go for a hike and spend some time outdoors, alone or with your family. You are almost guaranteed to come home with some interesting edibles. It is exciting to cook with new flavours that are available for only a few weeks each year. What is so special about foraging is that some types of mushrooms and plants can only be found in the wild; for many reasons they aren't suitable for commercial farming.

You do not necessarily have to go far to forage, either. It is quite common to find wild garlic mustard, wood sorrel, or wild berries growing in your backyard or a local park. I find mushrooms all the time while I'm walking my dog in the city. You just have to keep your eyes open and look. For the novice forager interested in learning, there are great field guides available, mycology and wild plant groups can be found online, and Google is always a handy reference. Just remember never to eat anything you are unsure of. It is always a good idea to forage with someone more experienced who can confirm a plant's identity.

My favourite thing to forage for is the morel mushroom. I have a love-hate relationship foraging for these choice edibles. The morel is the first mushroom I ever picked, so it has a sentimental hold on me. I was working at the Cataract Inn fifteen years ago in the spring when executive chef Graham Black strolled into the kitchen and showed me a handful of morels he'd found that morning. I was amazed. I thought mushrooms were bought in a store. As a kid, I had been warned about picking mushrooms, and rightfully so, as poisonous strains can be deadly. "Where did you find those?" I asked Graham. He told me they grow in partly shady, partly sunny, mossy, and slightly sandy soil. As it happened, the Cataract Inn was located across the road from a provincial park. Ever since I was a kid, I'd explored that park with friends, hiking, biking, camping, and at the odd bush party. I never expected my familiar backyard to now be my larder. That afternoon I grabbed a basket and ran into the valley to find some morels of my own. I came back having scored four pounds of black morels worth $100, a valuable haul for a young apprentice. I later learned there are three types of morels: black, grey, and gold. Black morels tend to grow in coniferous forest, under pine and cedar trees. Gold and grey grow under deciduous trees, particularly old crabapple and dead elm and poplar. Get a field guide or image-search the internet and get familiar with these mushrooms.

That was the love part of this relationship—the planting of the seed that awakened my soul to hunting and gathering. I went into the forest and came out with food—delicious, exotic, expensive mushrooms. I wasn't aware that I was incredibly lucky! Now here comes the hate part . . . I didn't know back then how elusive these little buggers could be. The morel is a fickle fungus, its growth determined by environment, temperature, moisture, and many other variables. Much to our sorrow, this mushroom has yet to be successfully cultivated, and that adds to the thrill of the hunt. Morels tend to grow in the same spot every year. The frustrating thing is that some years I will find twenty in one spot and other years just two. How happy do you think I am after driving an hour from the city to find just two mushrooms? However, it is what makes morels special: the hunt for something that only comes around for a few weeks once a year.

1. Amanita Jacksonii

2. Blackberries

3. Boletes

4. Chaga Mushroom

5. Chanterelles

6. Chicken of the Wood and Puffball

7. Lobster Mushroom

8. Morel

9. Pheasant Back

10. Saffron Caps

11. Shaggy Mane

1. Black Walnuts
2. Sumac
3. Wild Ginger
4. Cedar
5. Fiddleheads
6. Stinging Nettle

7. Wild Leeks
8. Wild Mint
9. Wild Watercress
10. Salmonberry
11. Pawpaw

Pickerel is a beautiful white freshwater lake fish. Subtle in flavour and flaky, it pairs well with creamy tartar sauce. Pickerel is one of my all-time favourite fish to catch and eat.

PICKEREL WITH POTATOES AND TARTAR SAUCE

Serves 4

Make the Tartar Sauce

In a food processor, pulse the egg and mustard to combine. With the processor running, very slowly pour the grapeseed oil, starting with a very thin stream, through the feed tube until all the oil is incorporated. You will see the oil start to emulsify with the egg, creating a thick mayonnaise. Add the lemon juice, capers, pickles, shallots, parsley, garlic, and a pinch each of salt and pepper. Pulse just to mix. (*The tartar sauce can be made ahead and stored, covered, in the fridge for up to 5 days.*)

Boil the Potatoes

In a small pot, cover the potatoes with water and add salt. Boil over high heat until fork-tender, 8 to 10 minutes. Drain and let cool slightly. Slice the potatoes into ¼-inch (5 mm) rounds and set aside.

Cook the Pickerel

Score the pickerel skin with a sharp knife to prevent the fillet from curling when searing. Season both sides of the fillets with salt.

Heat a large cast-iron skillet over high heat. Add the grapeseed oil and 1 tablespoon (15 mL) of the butter. Place the pickerel skin side down in the pan and sear until crispy on the bottom, 3 to 4 minutes. Do not move the fish; let the skin caramelize to prevent sticking to the pan. When the skin looks like it is starting to brown, carefully slide a thin metal spatula under the fillet without ripping the skin, turn the fillet, and cook the flesh side for 30 to 60 seconds. Finish by squeezing the lemon juice into the pan and remove from the heat.

Meanwhile, in a large skillet, melt the remaining 1 tablespoon (15 mL) butter over medium-high heat. Sauté the potatoes, green beans, and a pinch of salt, until the beans are fork-tender and the potatoes are warm, 2 to 3 minutes.

To serve, divide the fish, potatoes, and beans among plates. Top the fish with a generous spoonful of tartar sauce and garnish with fresh oregano.

TARTAR SAUCE

1 large egg

1 tablespoon (15 mL) Dijon mustard

1 cup (250 mL) grapeseed oil or vegetable oil

Juice of 1 lemon

¼ cup (60 mL) minced drained capers

¼ cup (60 mL) minced gherkin pickles

¼ cup (60 mL) minced shallot

¼ cup (60 mL) chopped fresh flat-leaf parsley

1 teaspoon (5 mL) minced garlic

Kosher salt and freshly cracked black pepper

PICKEREL WITH POTATOES

1 pound (450 g) mini potatoes

4 skin-on pickerel fillets (about 6 ounces/170 g each)

1 tablespoon (15 mL) grapeseed oil or vegetable oil

2 tablespoons (30 mL) unsalted butter, divided, for frying

1 lemon

1 pound (450 g) green beans, trimmed

Fresh oregano, for garnish

I had eaten pickerel as a kid and cooked it as a young chef, but I feel I truly ate pickerel for the first time when I was in my mid-twenties, when we cooked it in a cast-iron pan over a fire way up north while moose hunting one fall. It was pouring rain, and instead of hunting moose we decided we'd have better luck fishing in the lake. We hauled our legal limit for eight guys in about an hour—I have never caught so many fish so quickly. We dressed the fish, dusted the fillets with seasoned flour, fried them, sandwiched them inside fluffy white buns, and slathered them in mayo and hot sauce. Simple is sometimes the best way to truly taste your ingredients.

CAMPFIRE PICKEREL ON A BUN

Serves 6

Make the Buns

In a small saucepan, combine the milk, water, butter, and sugar. Heat just until lukewarm, stirring to melt the butter and dissolve the sugar. Remove from the heat. (Do not add yeast to hot liquid or it will kill the yeast and your dough will not rise.) Stir in the yeast and let sit for 3 minutes. The yeast should start to foam.

In a large bowl, stir together the flour and salt. Pour in the wet ingredients and mix by hand or on the lowest speed in a stand mixer for 10 minutes. Cover the bowl with plastic wrap or a kitchen towel and let the dough rise until doubled in size, 1 to 1½ hours.

Line a baking sheet with parchment paper. Scrape the dough onto a lightly floured work surface and divide into 6 equal pieces about the size of a golf ball. Cup your hand over a dough ball, with your fingertips and wrist on the work surface, and rotate your hand in a circular motion to shape the dough into a smooth ball. Evenly space the buns about 2 inches (5 cm) apart on the prepared baking sheet. Brush the buns with the egg wash. Place the baking sheet inside a large plastic bag and let the buns rise until doubled in size, 1 to 1½ hours. While the buns are rising, preheat the oven to 400°F (200°C).

Bake the buns until golden brown, 15 to 20 minutes. Let cool on a rack.

BUNS (MAKES 6 BUNS)

½ cup (125 mL) whole milk

½ cup (125 mL) water

2 tablespoons (30 mL) unsalted butter

1 tablespoon (15 mL) granulated sugar

¾ teaspoon (4 mL) active dry yeast

2½ cups (625 mL/300 g) all-purpose flour

1 teaspoon (5 mL) kosher salt

1 egg yolk beaten with

1 tablespoon (15 mL) water, for egg wash

recipe and ingredients continues

Make the Campfire Pickerel

Score the pickerel skin with a sharp knife to prevent the fillets from curling when searing.

In a medium bowl, whisk together the flour, paprika, garlic powder, salt, black pepper, and cayenne. Dredge the pickerel in the seasoned flour.

Heat a large cast-iron skillet over high heat. Add the grapeseed oil to the pan. Place the pickerel skin side down in the pan and sear until the skin is crispy, 2 to 3 minutes. Turn the fillets and cook for another 1 to 2 minutes, until both sides are crispy. Finish by squeezing the lemon over the fish in the pan and remove from the heat.

To serve, spread the tartar sauce on each bun, add a fillet of pickerel, and top with hot sauce and arugula.

CAMPFIRE PICKEREL

6 skin-on pickerel fillets (about 6 ounces/170 g each)
½ cup (125 mL) all-purpose flour
2 teaspoons (10 mL) smoked paprika
1 teaspoon (5 mL) garlic powder
1 teaspoon (5 mL) kosher salt
1 teaspoon (5 mL) black pepper
½ teaspoon (2 mL) cayenne pepper
2 tablespoons (30 mL) grapeseed oil, for frying
1 lemon

FOR SERVING

¾ cup (175 mL) Tartar Sauce (page 169)
Hot sauce
1½ cups (375 mL) baby arugula

Flipper pie is an eastern Canadian pie made with harp seal flipper. Highly regarded in Newfoundland tradition, flipper pie is quite similar to any meat pie—except for the main ingredient. Seal meat is a sustainable and renewable food that is very high in protein and iron, but it's controversial because it is a by-product of the fur trade. Seal hunting is a way of life for many Canadians and Indigenous people, and as such plays an important role in our culture.

This recipe was developed by my aunt who grew up in Newfoundland. If you enjoy fish dishes such as seafood chowders and fish stews, you will love the rich, flavourful taste of this one.

FLIPPER PIE

Makes 1 pie

Make the Filling

Bring a large pot of water to a boil with the vinegar and baking soda. Add the seal flippers, remove from the heat, and let the flippers soak for 1 hour to remove some of the fishy taste. Drain the flippers and rinse them well under cold running water.

Preheat the oven to 350°F (180°C).

In a large pot, brown the fatback over medium-high heat. Add the flippers and sear until brown on both sides. Add the stock, cover with a lid, transfer to the oven, and braise until the flippers are soft and the meat can be pulled away easily, about 1½ hours.

Remove the flippers from the pot. Remove and discard the bones. The meat usually breaks into chunks when removed from the bone, which is fine. Return the seal meat to the pot along with the turnip, onion, carrot, celery, thyme, salt, and pepper. Return to the oven and braise until the meat is fork-tender, 45 minutes. Remove from the oven and increase the oven temperature to 425°F (220°C).

Assemble the Pie

On a lightly floured work surface, gently roll out the larger disc of dough into a 12-inch (30 cm) circle that is ⅛-inch (3 mm) thick. Carefully lift one edge of the dough and roll the dough loosely around the rolling pin. Unroll the dough over a 9-inch (23 cm) pie plate. Gently press the dough into the pan and trim the edges flush with the pan. Roll out the smaller disc of dough for the top of the pie.

1 tablespoon (15 mL) white vinegar

1 tablespoon (15 mL) baking soda

2 harp seal flippers (about 1 pound/450 g each)

¾ cup (175 mL) diced pork fatback or bacon

3 cups (750 mL) homemade light game or chicken stock (see page 70)

1 cup (250 mL) peeled and diced turnip

½ cup (125 mL) diced white onion

½ cup (125 mL) peeled and diced carrot

½ cup (125 mL) diced celery

1 teaspoon (5 mL) chopped fresh thyme

1 teaspoon (5 mL) kosher salt

Freshly cracked black pepper

1 batch of Butter Pastry Dough (page 59)

1 egg yolk, lightly beaten, for egg wash

recipe and ingredients continues

Using a fork, gently prick the bottom of the pie shell multiple times in 1-inch (2.5 cm) increments. These small indents in the pastry will allow steam to escape and keep the pastry from rising. Scrape the filling into the pie shell and gently pat down. Brush the edges of the pastry with the egg wash. Carefully transfer the top layer of pastry onto the pie. Pinch the edges of the dough together to create a wavy pattern and seal the edges, or press with a fork around the edges to seal the top layer of pastry to the pie. Brush the top of the pie with the egg wash. Cut an X in the middle of the pie and randomly prick a few holes with a fork to allow steam to escape during baking. If you like, make decorations with scrap pieces of pastry.

Bake the pie for 5 minutes. Reduce the oven temperature to 350°F (180°C) and continue baking for 1 to 1½ hours. The crust should be a deep golden brown. Transfer the pie to a rack and let rest for 15 to 20 minutes before cutting and serving.

As a kid I used to fish in the pond in our backyard. There were mostly largemouth bass, but occasionally I would pull out a rainbow trout. It truly is a beautiful-looking fish. Trout has a mild delicate, flavour and juicy and fatty when not overcooked. The salty hint of the roe with the sweetness of the maple syrup is a great addition to this beautiful fish.

RAINBOW TROUT WITH ROE MAPLE BUTTER SAUCE

Serves 4

Roast the Vegetables

Position racks in the upper and lower thirds of the oven. Preheat the oven to 350°F (180°C).

Roast the sweet potatoes on a baking sheet lined with parchment paper until the outsides are caramelized, they are very soft, and their sugary liquid is coming out and bubbling on the baking sheet, about 1 hour. Let cool slightly, and then carefully peel off the skin, keeping the potatoes intact. Keep warm until ready to serve.

While the potatoes are roasting, cut the fennel bulbs lengthwise into wedges 1 inch (2.5 cm) thick, keeping a bit of the root intact so the layers stay together. Place the fennel wedges in a casserole dish and add the vegetable stock, beer, mustard, bay leaf, thyme, and salt and pepper to taste. Cover with foil and bake in the oven with the potatoes for 1 to 1½ hours or until the liquid is almost evaporated and the fennel is very soft.

Make the Roe Maple Butter Sauce

Meanwhile, in a small saucepan, combine the white wine, shallots, chili flakes, peppercorns, bay leaf, and thyme. Boil over high heat until only 1 to 2 tablespoons (15 to 30 mL) wine remain, 6 to 8 minutes. Add the cream and maple syrup and lower the heat to a simmer. Add 1 cube of butter and whisk until the butter is almost completely melted. Whisk in 2 more cubes of butter, and repeat until all the butter has been added and the sauce is emulsified. Stir in the lemon juice. Strain the sauce into a small saucepan. Stir in the trout roe and chives and keep warm.

recipe and ingredients continues

ROASTED VEGETABLES

3 unpeeled sweet potatoes
2 fennel bulbs, stalks removed
1 cup (250 mL) vegetable stock
1 bottle (12 ounces/355 mL) lager or ale
1 tablespoon (15 mL) grainy mustard
1 bay leaf
1 sprig fresh thyme
Kosher salt and black pepper

ROE MAPLE BUTTER SAUCE

1 cup (250 mL) dry white wine
1 tablespoon (15 mL) minced shallot
½ teaspoon (2 mL) red chili flakes
½ teaspoon (2 mL) black peppercorns
1 bay leaf
1 sprig fresh thyme
¼ cup (60 mL) heavy (35%) cream
2 tablespoons (30 mL) pure maple syrup
½ pound (225 g/1 cup/250 mL) cold unsalted butter, cut into cubes
Juice of 1 lemon
4 ounces (115 g) cured trout roe or salmon roe
¼ cup (60 mL) thinly sliced fresh chives

Cook the Trout

Season both sides of the fish with salt. Heat a large skillet over medium-high heat for 1 to 2 minutes, then add the grapeseed oil and butter. Place the trout skin side down in the pan and sear until the skin is crispy, 1 to 2 minutes. Turn the fish over and cook for 30 to 60 seconds. Squeeze the lemon juice into the pan and remove the fillets from the pan.

To serve, plate the sweet potatoes, fennel, and trout. Pour the roe maple butter sauce on top of the fish.

RAINBOW TROUT

4 skin-on rainbow trout fillets (6 ounces/170 g each)

Kosher salt

1 tablespoon (15 mL) each grapeseed oil or vegetable oil and unsalted butter, for sautéing

1 lemon

My first job was cooking at a breakfast diner at the age of thirteen, and because of that I love brunch. In my opinion, a good brunch is just as important as lunch or dinner. This recipe will surely impress your family or guests. The homemade smoked salmon is what makes this dish, and served with perfectly poached eggs, a classic hollandaise sauce, and home fries, it is such a treat. Serve with a green salad.

SMOKED SALMON EGGS BENEDICT

Serves 4

In a small saucepan over high heat, combine the white wine, shallot, and bay leaf. Boil over high heat until the wine is reduced to 2 tablespoons (30 mL), about 5 minutes. Strain, reserving the liquid. Rinse and dry the pan.

In the same pan, melt the butter over high heat and boil for 1 minute. Reduce the heat to low and simmer until the foam rises to the surface and the butter begins to brown on the bottom. Be careful not to let the bottom burn. Remove from the heat. This is your clarified butter.

In a medium stainless steel bowl set over a saucepan of simmering water, whisk the egg yolks with the wine reduction for 3 to 4 minutes, until the mixture is light and frothy and has reached the ribbon stage—when you lift the whisk, the eggs should fall back into the bowl in ribbons that slowly merge back into the mixture. Remove the bowl from the heat. While whisking vigorously, drizzle ¼ cup (60 mL) of the clarified butter into the mixture. Repeat until all the butter is added, including any small brown bits from the bottom, and the hollandaise is emulsified. The sauce should be light and fluffy. Stir in ½ teaspoon (2 mL) of the salt, ½ teaspoon (2 mL) of the pepper, and the lemon juice. Cover and keep warm.

In a medium pot, cover the mini potatoes with water and boil until fork-tender, about 10 minutes. Drain the potatoes, return them to the pot, and lightly crush them. Do not mash them.

Heat a large skillet over high heat and add the grapeseed oil. Add the crushed potatoes, season with 1 teaspoon (5 mL) of the salt and the remaining ½ teaspoon (2 mL) pepper, and fry, turning occasionally, until the potato are crispy, about 5 minutes.

½ cup (125 mL) dry white wine

1 tablespoon (15 mL) minced shallot

1 bay leaf

1 cup (250 mL) unsalted butter

3 egg yolks

3 teaspoons (15 mL) kosher salt, divided

1 teaspoon (5 mL) freshly ground black pepper, divided

Juice of ½ lemon

1 pound (450 g) mini red potatoes

2 tablespoons (30 mL) grapeseed oil or vegetable oil

½ cup (125 mL) vinegar

8 eggs

16 slices of Smoked Wild Salmon (page 184)

4 English muffins, toasted

½ cup (125 mL) sliced green onion (white and light green parts only), for serving

recipe and ingredients continues

Fill a large pot about two-thirds with water and bring to a simmer over medium heat. Add the vinegar and the remaining 1½ teaspoons (7 mL) salt. Gently crack the eggs into a medium bowl. Spin the water with a slotted spoon. (This gives the eggs more of an oval shape and keeps the whites intact.) Tip the bowl, then slowly, and carefully slide the eggs, all at the same time, into the simmering water. Poach for 2 to 3 minutes, until the whites are cooked but the yolks are still soft. Using the slotted spoon, lift the eggs out of the water. Blot the water off the bottom of spoon onto a kitchen towel or paper towel.

Lay 2 slices of smoked salmon on each toasted muffin half and top with a poached egg. Spoon the warm hollandaise sauce over each egg. Serve with the home fries and garnish with sliced green onions.

I love the sweetness of maple syrup with the richness of fresh wild B.C. spring salmon. The fish are in season right after I have made maple syrup in the spring, and so are local asparagus and chives.

MAPLE-GLAZED SALMON WITH CHIVE BUTTER SAUCE

Serves 4

Make the Chive Butter Sauce

In a small saucepan, combine the white wine, shallot, thyme, bay leaf, chili flakes, and pepper. Boil over high heat until only 1 to 2 tablespoons (15 to 30 mL) of liquid remain. Add the cream and lower the heat to a simmer. Add 1 cube of butter and whisk until the butter is almost completely melted. Whisk in 2 more cubes of butter, and repeat until all the butter has been added and the sauce is emulsified. Stir in the lemon juice. Strain the sauce into a small saucepan and keep warm.

Make the Maple-Glazed Salmon

Heat a large skillet over high heat. Season both sides of the salmon with the salt. Add the butter and grapeseed oil to the pan. Place the salmon skin side down in the skillet and cook, without moving the fish, until the skin is caramelized and crispy, 3 to 4 minutes. Turn the fish and reduce the heat to low. Squeeze the lemon juice into the pan and add the maple syrup. Turn the fish again so that it is skin side down, then tilt the pan to one side and, using a serving spoon, scoop the maple syrup and baste the fish continually for 1 minute. The hot syrup will reduce slightly and give the fish a nice glaze.

Sauté the Asparagus

Heat a second large skillet over high heat. Add the butter and asparagus and sauté for 2 to 3 minutes, until tender.

To serve, whisk the chives into the warm butter sauce. Serve the salmon with the asparagus and spoon the chive butter sauce onto the plate.

CHIVE BUTTER SAUCE

1 cup (250 mL) dry white wine
1 tablespoon (15 mL) minced
 shallot
2 sprigs fresh thyme
1 bay leaf
½ teaspoon (2 mL) red chili flakes
Freshly cracked black pepper
2 tablespoons (30 mL) heavy
 (35%) cream
½ pound (225 g/1 cup/250 mL)
 cold unsalted butter, cut into
 ½-inch (1 cm) cubes
Juice of 1 lemon
2 tablespoons (30 mL) thinly
 sliced fresh chives

MAPLE-GLAZED SALMON

4 skin-on salmon fillets (about
 6 ounces/170 g each)
1 teaspoon (5 mL) kosher salt
1 tablespoon (15 mL) unsalted
 butter, for frying
2 tablespoons (30 mL) grapeseed
 oil or vegetable oil, for frying
1 lemon
½ cup (125 mL) pure maple syrup

SAUTÉED ASPARAGUS

1 tablespoon (15 mL) unsalted
 butter
1½ pounds (675 g) fresh spring
 asparagus, trimmed

Smoking salmon is a wonderful way to preserve your catch. Smoked salmon eggs Benedict is a brunch favourite at Antler, but this salmon is also great as an appetizer or in a sandwich.

If you do not have a commercial smoker, you can rig one up in your oven with foil and wood chips—or simply omit the smoking process and make the unsmoked cured salmon referred to as gravlax.

SMOKED WILD SALMON

Makes 1 large fillet

Remove any pin bones from the salmon. In a small bowl, stir together the salt, brown sugar, fennel seeds, caraway seeds and dill seeds (if using), and pepper. Place the salmon in a casserole dish. Cover evenly with the salt mixture. Cover and let cure in the fridge for 4 to 5 days. The fish should feel firm to the touch.

Wipe off the excess cure with a damp kitchen towel or rinse under cold running water and pat dry. Set the smoker to the lowest setting and smoke the salmon with a cold plate attachment or over ice for 20 minutes. Turn off the heat, close the vent, and let the salmon sit in the smoker for 1 hour before opening.

Cool the salmon in the fridge for at least 1 hour before slicing. Store in an airtight container or wrapped in plastic wrap in the fridge for up to 1 week or in the freezer for up to 8 months.

1 wild salmon fillet
   (2½ pounds/1.125 kg)
1 cup (250 mL) kosher salt (I use
   Diamond Crystal)
1 cup (250 mL) brown sugar
1 tablespoon (15 mL) fennel
   seeds
1 teaspoon (5 mL) caraway seeds
   (optional)
1 teaspoon (5 mL) dill seeds
   (optional)
1 teaspoon (5 mL) freshly ground
   black pepper

The sweet flavour of scallops with salty, fatty bacon is a classic combination. This is my take on the classic French choucroute garnie, a delicious bacon, cabbage, and wine stew.

SEARED SCALLOPS WITH BACON AND CABBAGE

Serves 4 to 6

Make the Apple Cider–Braised Red Cabbage Purée

In a large pot, combine the red cabbage, apple cider, cinnamon stick, cloves, and salt. Bring to a boil over high heat, then reduce the heat to the lowest setting, cover with a lid, and simmer, stirring occasionally, until all the liquid has evaporated, about 1 hour. Discard the cinnamon stick. In a high-speed blender, purée the cabbage until smooth. Return the purée to the pot and cover with a lid to keep warm.

Make the Choucroute

In a large pot over medium heat, cook the bacon until it begins to crisp, 5 to 8 minutes. Add the onion and cook for 3 minutes. Add the garlic, green cabbage, white wine, thyme, juniper, and pepper. Reduce the heat to low and cook, stirring occasionally, until the cabbage is very soft and tender and the liquid has evaporated, 15 to 20 minutes. Check the seasoning and add a pinch of salt if needed. Be careful not to over-season; there may be enough salt in the bacon. Remove from the heat and cover with a lid to keep warm.

Sear the Scallops

Heat a large cast-iron or other heavy skillet over high heat for 4 to 5 minutes. Season the scallops with salt. Add the grapeseed oil to the pan. Add the scallops to the pan and then add the butter. Sear the scallops, without moving them, for 2 to 3 minutes, until they caramelize and get a deep brown crust. When they are golden around the edges, flip the scallops and cook for 30 to 60 seconds, just to heat through. Scallops are best eaten medium-rare doneness, when they are plump and juicy. Reheat the purée if needed before serving.

Serve the scallops with the red cabbage purée and green cabbage.

APPLE CIDER–BRAISED RED CABBAGE PURÉE

4 cups (1 L) thinly sliced red cabbage (½ medium cabbage)
4 cups (1 L) fresh apple cider
1 cinnamon stick
1 teaspoon (5 mL) ground cloves
½ teaspoon (2 mL) kosher salt

CHOUCROUTE

1 pound (450 g) Wild Boar Bacon (page 87) or slab bacon, diced
1 cup (250 mL) thinly sliced white onion
2 teaspoons (10 mL) minced garlic
8 cups (2 L) thinly sliced green cabbage (1 medium cabbage)
1 cup (250 mL) dry white wine
1 teaspoon (5 mL) chopped fresh thyme
½ teaspoon (2 mL) ground fresh juniper berries
Freshly cracked black pepper
Kosher salt

SCALLOPS

12 large (U10) sea scallops
Kosher salt
1 tablespoon (15 mL) each grapeseed oil or vegetable oil and unsalted butter, for searing

I caught live Dungeness crab for the first time a few years ago. I thought I knew what fresh crab tasted like from working in restaurants that had them flown in. They were tasty, but they were nothing compared with the crabs I caught and ate within two hours. These had a rich sweetness with a hint of the sea—heavenly. When you start with amazing ingredients, you do not need to do much to them, they taste so great on their own. These crabs are messy, and it's a pain to get at the meat, but it is so worth it. Anyway, half the fun is getting messy with your friends and family while sharing crab!

Always check fishing regulations and seasons before harvesting.

STEAMED DUNGENESS CRABS

Serves 5

Pour about 1 inch (2.5 cm) of water into a large stockpot and add the white wine and a little salt. Bring to a boil over high heat. Add the crabs to the pot, cover with a lid, and steam for 6 to 8 minutes, until the crabs are bright red and a probe thermometer inserted into the body of a crab reads 165°F (74°C). Remove the crabs using long tongs and arrange on a platter.

Meanwhile, in a small saucepan over medium heat, melt the butter. Add the garlic and cook for 1 minute. Pour the garlic butter into a large ramekin and prepare to get messy.

When serving, instruct your guests to crack open the claws, legs, and shells, extract the flaky meat with your fingers or crab forks, and dip the meat into the butter. Inside the large body shell there is delicious roe and wonderful-tasting liquid. Do not eat the gills (the fuzzy-looking things on the sides).

1 cup (250 mL) dry white wine
Kosher salt
5 live Dungeness crabs
½ cup (125 mL) unsalted butter
1 tablespoon (15 mL) minced garlic

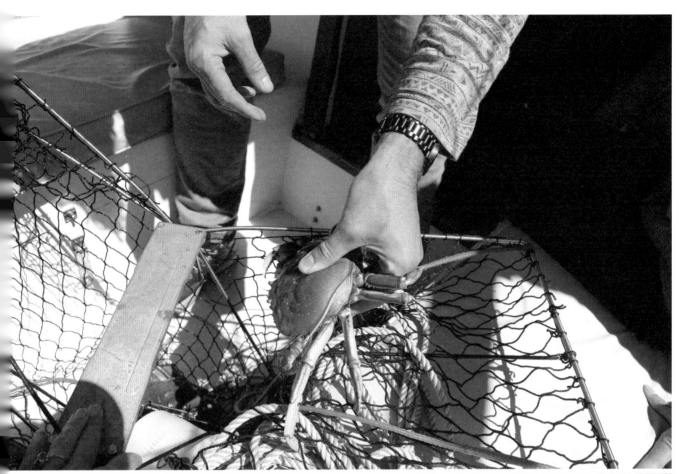

Canada is home to beautiful seafood along our coasts, but the only shrimp I saw growing up and cooking in my early culinary career were frozen tiger shrimp from Asia. It is a shame that we rely on foreign food just because it's cheap. Shrimp from warmer climates grow faster and are market ready in a matter of months, whereas Canadian shrimp take about four years to grow to a similar size in our cold water.

Spot prawns are wild-caught off the coast of British Columbia and are large, fat, red shrimp with white spots. They have a tender sweet-salty flavour and are by far one of my favourites. One of the best ways to eat them is grilled fresh in their shell over an open wood or charcoal fire. With garlic butter, of course.

GRILLED SPOT PRAWNS

Serves 4 to 6

If you are using wooden skewers, soak them in water overnight to prevent them from burning.

Light a charcoal or gas grill and preheat for 10 minutes. Skewer the prawns lengthwise so they don't curl. Drizzle the prawns with olive oil and season with the salt and pepper. Grill them for 1 to 2 minutes per side.

In a small saucepan on the grill, melt the butter. Add the garlic and cook for 1 minute.

To serve, pour the garlic butter over the prawns and sprinkle with the green onions and cilantro.

2 pounds (900 g) extra-large (15–20 per pound) spot prawns
Olive oil, for drizzling
1 teaspoon (5 mL) kosher salt
Freshly cracked black pepper
½ cup (125 mL) unsalted butter
2 tablespoons (30 mL) minced garlic
½ cup (125 mL) chopped green onion (white and light green parts only)
½ cup (125 mL) chopped fresh cilantro

I am incredibly spoiled to have twice had the chance to go fishing for prawns on a commercial boat. Eating a prawn raw right out of the ocean is one of my all-time most memorable food moments. I was instructed to pull off the head and suck out the brains. It tasted like sea urchin, but the legs were still moving—kind of freaky. I peeled back the shell from the tail and discovered that's the best way to eat raw prawns! The flavour of fresh prawns is sweet and delicate—a special seasonal treat. A ceviche is the perfect way to showcase their natural flavour.

Fresh prawns are bright red all over. If any part of the head is black, the meat has started to deteriorate. Do not eat them raw.

SPOT PRAWN CEVICHE

Serves 6 as an appetizer

Peel and devein the prawns. Remove the heads and reserve for garnish (optional). (You can save the shells to make stock.) Cut the prawns into ½-inch (1 cm) chunks. In a large bowl, combine the prawns, lemon and lime juice, olive oil, red peppers, shallots, cilantro, jalapeño (if using), salt, and black pepper. Mix well and serve immediately. Instruct your guests to suck the brains from the heads.

2 pounds (900 g) extra-large (15–20 per pound) spot prawns
Juice of 2 lemons
Juice of 2 limes
½ cup (125 mL) olive oil
½ cup (125 mL) diced red bell pepper
¼ cup (60 mL) minced shallot
1 tablespoon (15 mL) chopped fresh cilantro
1 tablespoon (15 mL) minced jalapeño pepper with seeds (optional)
1 teaspoon (5 mL) kosher salt
Freshly cracked black pepper

Sablefish, also known as black cod (although it's not part of the cod family), is a rich and succulent white fish with a buttery texture found off the coast of British Columbia and Alaska. The whipped cod purée, also called montecato, is a luscious and rich addition to the fish and crispy top of the potato galette.

SABLEFISH WITH WHIPPED COD PURÉE AND POTATO GALETTE

Serves 6

Make the Potato Galette

Preheat the oven to 375°F (190°C). Line the bottom of a 9- × 5-inch (2 L) loaf pan with parchment paper and brush the bottom and sides with melted butter.

Using a mandoline or food processor fitted with the slicing disc, thinly slice the potatoes. Layer the potatoes in the pan, brushing with the melted butter and seasoning with the salt, thyme, and nutmeg between layers. Cover with foil and bake until the potatoes are soft when poked with a fork, 1 to 1½ hours. Remove the foil and bake for an additional 15 to 20 minutes, until the top is golden. Let cool slightly before cutting into 6 slices.

Make the Whipped Cod Purée

In a medium saucepan, combine the soaked cod, potatoes, garlic, and milk. Bring to a simmer over medium heat, whisking occasionally, and simmer until the potatoes are soft, 10 to 15 minutes. Strain, reserving the milk and solids separately. In a food processor, purée the potato and cod mixture. With the processor running, slowly add the reserved milk and the olive oil in a thin stream until all the liquid is incorporated. Keep warm.

Cook the Sablefish

Heat a large skillet over medium heat. Season the sablefish with salt. Add the grapeseed oil and the butter to the pan. Place the fish in the pan skin side down and sear, without moving, until the skin is crispy, 3 to 5 minutes. Turn the fish and cook for 1 to 2 minutes more, until it is cooked through. Remove the fish from the pan and loosely cover with foil to keep warm. Wipe out the pan with paper towel.

POTATO GALETTE

½ cup (125 mL) unsalted butter, melted, more for the pan
1 pound (450 g) russet potatoes, peeled
2 teaspoons (10 mL) kosher salt
1 teaspoon (5 mL) chopped fresh thyme
½ teaspoon (2 mL) nutmeg

WHIPPED COD PURÉE

¼ pound (115 g) salt cod, soaked in water for 24 hours
¼ pound (115 g) peeled and diced white potatoes
4 cloves garlic
1½ cups (375 mL) whole milk
2 tablespoons (30 mL) olive oil

SABLEFISH

6 skin-on sablefish fillets (5.5 ounces/150 g each)
Kosher salt
1 tablespoon (15 mL) grapeseed oil or vegetable oil, for cooking
1 tablespoon (15 mL) unsalted butter, for cooking

Sauté the Broccoli

In the same pan, over high heat, then add the olive oil, and butter, then the broccoli. Season with salt and pepper and cook, stirring occasionally, for 2 to 3 minutes or until fork-tender.

Serve the sablefish topped with whipped cod purée, with a slice of potato galette and broccoli alongside.

SAUTÉED BROCCOLI

2 tablespoons (30 mL) olive oil, for sautéing

1 tablespoon (15 mL) unsalted butter, for sautéing

2 bunches broccoli, cut into florets

2 teaspoons (10 mL) kosher salt

Freshly cracked black pepper

Fish and chips is my ultimate gluttonous treat. Perch fillets are the perfect size for quick frying in beer batter. The homemade tartar sauce is rich and creamy, the perfect accompaniment to the crispy fish and potato wedges.

Yellow perch is a white-fleshed freshwater fish native to the Great Lakes and surrounding lakes and streams in Canada and the United States. It is one of North America's most popular freshwater fish, being commercially harvested for over a century.

It is important to use a deep-fry thermometer when deep-frying because vegetable oil will catch fire above 450°F (230°C).

PERCH FISH AND CHIPS

Serves 4 to 6

Heat the vegetable oil in a large pot over high heat until it reaches 300°F (150°C), then reduce the heat to medium.

Line a baking sheet with paper towel. Working in batches, blanch the potatoes in the hot oil until tender in the centre but not yet turning colour, 3 to 5 minutes. Remove the potatoes from the hot oil with tongs and lay them on the baking sheet. Heat the oil to 350°F (180°C) and hold at that temperature.

In a medium bowl, whisk together the egg, half of the beer, the flour, garlic powder, paprika, and 2 tablespoons (30 mL) of the salt. While whisking, slowly pour in the remaining beer, whisking until the batter comes together. Dip the perch fillets in the batter. Carefully place 4 fillets in the hot oil and fry until golden, 3 to 5 minutes per side. Using tongs, remove the fillets from the hot oil and drain on paper towel. Repeat to cook the remaining 4 fillets.

Working in batches, deep-fry the potatoes until golden brown and crispy, about 4 minutes. Remove with tongs and season with the remaining 1 tablespoon (15 mL) salt.

Serve the fish with the chips, tartar sauce, and lemon wedges.

8 cups (2 L) vegetable oil, for frying

1½ pounds (675 g) unpeeled yellow potatoes (about 3 large potatoes), cut into thick wedges

1 egg

1 bottle (12 ounces/355 mL) lager or pilsner beer, divided

1 cup (250 mL) all-purpose flour

1 tablespoon (15 mL) garlic powder

1 tablespoon (15 mL) smoked paprika

3 tablespoons (45 mL) kosher salt, divided

8 skinless perch fillets (4 ounces/115 g each)

1 cup (250 mL) Tartar Sauce (page 169)

1 lemon cut into wedges, for garnish

Halibut is a delicious rich, tender, flaky white fish, delicate in flavour. Very low in fat, so be careful not to overcook halibut or it will be dry. Creamy polenta is a great pairing with this fish because of the subtle texture of the fish and the richness of polenta. Wild leeks (ramps) are in season during halibut season, so this is a natural combination. The nuttiness of the hazelnuts matched with the punch of the wild leeks makes a great topping.

HALIBUT WITH CREAMY POLENTA AND WILD LEEKS

Serves 6

Make the Creamy Polenta

In a medium pot, combine the milk, cream, and salt. Bring to a simmer over medium heat, then whisk in the polenta in a steady stream. Reduce the heat to low and cook, stirring every 3 to 5 minutes, making sure to scrape the bottom of the pot to prevent scorching, until the polenta resembles thick porridge, 30 to 40 minutes. Remove from the heat and stir in the Parmesan and butter. Keep warm.

Make the Hazelnut Crumble

Separate the white bulbs of the leeks from the green tops. Set aside the bulbs. Thinly slice enough of the green tops to measure 2 tablespoons (30 mL) and set aside the remaining tops.

In a small bowl, stir together the sliced leek tops, hazelnuts, and orange zest. Set aside.

Cook the Halibut

Season both sides of the halibut with salt and pepper. Heat a large skillet over medium-high heat. Add the olive oil. Place the fish in the pan and fry until golden and crispy, 2 to 3 minutes. Turn the fish over, squeeze the lemon juice into the pan, add the butter, and cook the fish for another 1 to 2 minutes or until tender. Remove the fish from the pan.

In the same pan (no need to wipe it out) over medium-high heat, sauté the reserved wild leek bulbs for 1 to 2 minutes. Add the reserved green tops, stir, and cook until wilted, about 1 minute.

To serve, spoon the polenta onto warmed plates and top with the wild leeks and halibut. Top the halibut with the hazelnut crumble. Garnish the plate with the wild leek pesto.

CREAMY POLENTA

2 cups (500 mL) whole milk

1½ cups (375 mL) heavy (35%) cream

1 tablespoon (15 mL) kosher salt

½ cup (125 mL) instant polenta

½ cup (125 mL) freshly grated Parmesan cheese

½ cup (125 mL) unsalted butter, cut into cubes

HAZELNUT CRUMBLE

1 pound (450 g) wild leeks, trimmed

½ cup (125 mL) chopped toasted hazelnuts

1 tablespoon (15 mL) orange zest

HALIBUT

6 skinless halibut fillets (5.5 ounces/150 g each)

1 teaspoon (5 mL) kosher salt

Freshly cracked black pepper

1 tablespoon (15 mL) olive oil

1 lemon

1 tablespoon (15 mL) unsalted butter

¼ cup (60 mL) Wild Leek Pesto (page 228), for garnish

Arctic char hails from the northern region of Canada and is similar in taste and texture to trout and salmon. The fat, oil, and omega-3 content of the fish is increased by the icy water they live in, resulting in a firmer texture and more complex flavour. Arctic char is in season in August through late fall, at the same time that saffron milk cap mushrooms are popping up in the coniferous forests. Bright orange in colour, these mushrooms are high in beta-carotene and typically grow in abundance, making them fun (and easy) to pick. Saffron caps have a firm texture and pair nicely with the delicate texture of the fish. They grow under spruce trees and have a natural forest taste that complements the mild flavour of the Arctic char.

Arctic char can be served a bit rare, but I suggest not cooking more than medium doneness.

ARCTIC CHAR WITH SAFFRON MILK CAP MUSHROOMS AND PEPPER COULIS

Serves 4

Using a gas burner, barbecue, or broiler, grill the whole sweet peppers until the skin is black on all sides. Place the peppers in a bowl and cover with plastic wrap. The heat from the peppers will steam them, making the black skin easier to remove. When the peppers have cooled, peel and rinse them. Remove and discard the seeds. In a small food processor, purée the yellow pepper. The coulis should be smooth and sweet tasting. Add a little olive oil and salt to adjust flavour and consistency, if needed. Transfer to a small bowl. Rinse clean the bowl of the food processor. Repeat to make a red pepper coulis.

Heat a large skillet over high heat and add 1 tablespoon (15 mL) of the butter and 1 tablespoon (15 mL) of the grapeseed oil. Add the mushrooms, season with salt and pepper, and sauté until softened and tender, 3 to 4 minutes. Remove from the heat and keep warm.

In a medium skillet over high heat, sauté the peas in 1 tablespoon (15 mL) of the butter until tender, 2 to 3 minutes. Remove from the heat and keep warm.

Season both sides of the Arctic char with salt. Heat a large skillet over medium-high heat and add the remaining 1 tablespoon (15 mL) grapeseed oil. Add the fish skin side down and sear until the skin is crispy, about 2 minutes. Add the remaining 1 tablespoon (15 mL) butter to the pan, turn the fish, and squeeze the lemon juice into the pan. Cook for 1 to 2 minutes more, until the flesh side is cooked and no longer appears raw and fleshy. Remove from the pan.

To serve, spoon the red and yellow pepper coulis, one at a time, onto plates. Arrange the fish, peas, and mushrooms on top.

1 yellow bell pepper

1 red bell pepper

2 tablespoons (30 mL) olive oil (optional)

3 tablespoons (45 mL) unsalted butter, divided

2 tablespoons (30 mL) grapeseed oil or vegetable oil, divided

1 pound (450 g) saffron milk cap mushrooms, brushed clean and cut in half (chanterelles or shiitake can be substituted)

1 teaspoon (5 mL) kosher salt

Freshly cracked black pepper

½ pound (225 g) freshly shucked sweet peas

4 skin-on Arctic char fillets (6 ounces/170 g each)

1 lemon

At Antler we make this dish in the fall, when lobster mushrooms are in season. Lobster mushrooms have an uncanny resemblance to lobster in colour, smell, and taste. Your guests will not believe this bisque does not contain any shellfish.

Fresh mushrooms are ideal, but dried can be used, although their flavour is not as intense. Fresh lobster mushrooms can be quite dirty. The best way to clean them is with a small brush or a toothbrush. If they are very dirty, a gentle rinse with water and a wipe with paper towel also works well. Pernod is the classic ingredient finishing the true lobster bisque with a hint of anise flavour. The rich and creamy foam topping is a decadent finishing touch.

LOBSTER MUSHROOM BISQUE

Serves 6

Make the Bisque

In a large pot, heat the olive oil over medium heat. Add the mushrooms, onion, carrot, and celery and cook, stirring occasionally, until the onions are translucent and tender, 8 to 10 minutes. Add the salt, chili flakes, bay leaf, vegetable stock, tomatoes and their juice, tomato paste, milk, and cream. Simmer, uncovered and stirring occasionally, until the vegetables and mushrooms are very soft, 30 to 45 minutes.

Working in batches, purée the soup in a high-speed blender. Taste and adjust seasoning if needed. Strain the soup through a fine-mesh sieve to achieve the desired velvety texture, pressing on the solids with a ladle in a circular motion. Return the soup to the pot and stir in the Pernod. Keep warm over low heat while you make the foam.

Make the Creamy Tomato Parmesan Foam

In a small saucepan over medium-high heat, whisk together the cream, tomato paste, and Parmesan. When hot, remove from the heat. Using an immersion blender or electric beater, blend on high speed until frothy.

To serve, ladle the soup into warmed bowls and spoon the foam on top.

BISQUE

½ cup (125 mL) olive oil

2½ pounds (1.125 kg) fresh lobster mushrooms, cleaned and roughly chopped

2 cups (500 mL) chopped white onion (about 2 medium onions)

1 cup (250 mL) chopped carrot

1 cup (250 mL) chopped celery

1 teaspoon (5 mL) kosher salt

Pinch of red chili flakes

1 bay leaf

2 cups (500 mL) vegetable stock

2 cups (500 mL) canned whole tomatoes

¼ cup (60 mL) tomato paste

2 cups (500 mL) whole milk

2 cups (500 mL) heavy (35%) cream

¼ cup (60 mL) Pernod

CREAMY TOMATO PARMESAN FOAM

½ cup (125 mL) heavy (35%) cream

1 tablespoon (15 mL) tomato paste

1 tablespoon (15 mL) freshly grated Parmesan cheese

Stinging nettles grow wild in abundance all over North America in sunny, moist soil along streams, rivers, lakes, fencerows, and fields from spring into early summer. The best time to harvest them is in the spring, when the leaves are most tender. If you've never walked through a patch of nettles, consider yourself very lucky, because they burn like hell. When foraging and preparing nettles, wear thick gloves and a jacket or thick sweater to protect your arms.

So why eat these, you might be wondering. Nettles lose their sting when they're cooked or dried. They are packed full of iron, vitamin C, vitamin A, and magnesium. They can be enjoyed sautéed like spinach or made into a pasta stuffing or pressed into the pasta dough itself. In this recipe, I incorporate them into a healthy green soup. It is important to use good-quality extra-virgin olive oil in this recipe for its superior flavour as a finishing touch that's drizzled on the soup just before serving.

STINGING NETTLE SOUP

Serves 6 to 8

While wearing gloves, wash, drain, and pat dry the stinging nettle leaves. In a large pot, melt the butter over medium heat. Add the nettle leaves and cook, stirring frequently, until wilted, 2 to 3 minutes. (Like spinach leaves, they will shrink considerably.) Using tongs, transfer the nettle leaves to a medium bowl and set aside.

Return the pot to medium heat. Add the onion, celery, garlic, thyme, salt, and pepper to taste. Cook for 3 minutes. Add the potatoes, bay leaves, and vegetable stock and simmer until the potatoes are soft, 20 to 30 minutes.

Discard the bay leaves. Add the nettle leaves to the soup. Using an immersion blender or in a high-speed blender, purée the soup until smooth, adding the cream while blending. Strain back into the pot.

Ladle the soup into warmed bowls and drizzle with the olive oil.

8 cups (2 L) fresh stinging nettle leaves

¼ cup (60 mL) unsalted butter

1 cup (250 mL) chopped white onion

½ cup (125 mL) chopped celery

1 tablespoon (15 mL) minced garlic

1 teaspoon (5 mL) fresh thyme leaves

2 teaspoons (10 mL) kosher salt

Freshly cracked black pepper

3 cups (750 mL) peeled and diced white potato

2 bay leaves

6 cups (1.5 L) vegetable or light game bird stock (see page 70; light chicken stock can be used)

½ cup (125 mL) heavy (35%) cream

Extra-virgin olive oil, for drizzling

Wild leeks, or ramps, have a sweet garlic and onion flavour that pairs nicely with the earthy flavour of potato. Enriched with crème fraîche and the salty hint of the caviar, this is a beautifully balanced and comforting soup that can be served hot or cold like a classic vichyssoise.

WILD LEEK AND POTATO SOUP WITH CAVIAR AND CRÈME FRAÎCHE

Serves 4 to 6

In a large pot, melt the butter over medium heat, then add the olive oil. Add the leek bulbs, onion, celery, and salt and cook, stirring occasionally, for about 3 minutes. Stir in the garlic and potatoes. Add the white wine and vegetable stock. Reduce the heat to low and simmer, uncovered and stirring occasionally, until the potatoes are very soft, 30 to 45 minutes.

Using an immersion blender or high-speed blender, purée the soup until smooth, 2 to 3 minutes, pouring in the cream in a slow, steady stream while blending. Strain the soup back into the pot to remove any lumps or fibre. Adjust the seasoning, if needed.

Pour the soup into warmed bowls and garnish with the crème fraîche, caviar, wild leek greens, and a drizzle of olive oil.

2 tablespoons (30 mL) unsalted butter
2 tablespoons (30 mL) olive oil
1½ cups (375 mL) sliced wild leek bulbs
½ cup (125 mL) chopped white onion
1 cup (250 mL) chopped celery
2 teaspoons (10 mL) kosher salt
1 tablespoon (15 mL) minced garlic
4 cups (1 L) peeled and chopped white potato
½ cup (125 mL) dry white wine
4 cups (1 L) vegetable or light game bird stock (see page 70; light chicken stock can be used)
1 cup (250 mL) heavy (35%) cream

GARNISH

¼ cup (60 mL) crème fraîche
1 tin (1 ounce/28 g) sturgeon caviar
½ cup (125 mL) thinly sliced wild leek greens
Extra-virgin olive oil, for drizzling

Shaggy mane mushrooms are very common in grassy fields, along hiking paths, on golf courses, and even in your backyard in the city. They have a wonderful rich butter flavour compared with store-bought mushrooms. Another fun fact about these mushrooms is that they are in the ink cap family of mushrooms, meaning that as they mature, they melt and turn into black mush. (That's the reason you will never see them for sale in a store or at the market.) After picking, shaggy manes need to be cooked within twenty-four hours.

This recipe is just as tasty with any wild mushrooms that are available to you. Even white button mushrooms will work!

CREAM OF SHAGGY MANE MUSHROOM SOUP

Serves 6

In a medium pot over medium heat, melt the butter. Add the mushrooms and onion and cook for 5 minutes, stirring occasionally, allowing the moisture to come out of the mushrooms and reduce a little. Add the garlic, thyme, bay leaves, salt, and pepper to taste; stir to combine. Add the cream, and stock and bring to a simmer over low heat; simmer until the mushrooms and onions are very tender and the liquid has visibly reduced, 25 to 20 minutes.

Discard the bay leaves. Using an immersion blender or high-speed blender, purée the soup.

Ladle the soup into warmed bowls and garnish with chopped chives and drizzle with olive oil. Serve with the crostini.

¼ cup (60 mL) unsalted butter
¾ pound (340 g) shaggy mane mushrooms, washed and dried
1 cup (250 mL) chopped white onion
2 tablespoons (30 mL) minced garlic
1 teaspoon (5 mL) chopped fresh thyme
2 bay leaves
1 teaspoon (5 mL) kosher salt
Freshly cracked black pepper
3 cups (750 mL) light chicken or game stock (see page 70)
1 cup (250 mL) heavy (35%) cream

GARNISH
Chopped fresh chives
1 tablespoon (15 mL) extra-virgin olive oil
Baguette crostini (optional)

A lot of my ideas for recipes come from my time in the woods. I was foraging for mushrooms one day and realized they were growing on the forest floor but completely blanketed in pine needles. I remembered learning about Indigenous cultures drinking pine needle tea, so I thought of using these two ingredients together in a dish. The earthy taste of mushroom and hint of forest from the pine are incredible together.

Pine needles have an interesting lemony flavour and are full of vitamin C. In fact, some varieties have four to five times more vitamin C than oranges. Do some simple tree identification research before you head out to harvest pine needles, because a few species of pine are mildly toxic.

PINE NEEDLE BROTH WITH WILD MUSHROOMS

Serves 4 to 6

In a medium pot, combine the venison stock, pine needles, thyme, bay leaves, peppercorns, and ½ teaspoon (2 mL) of the salt. Bring to a gentle simmer over medium heat and simmer for 6 to 8 minutes. Do not let the broth boil or it will become cloudy. Keep hot over low heat while you sauté the mushrooms.

In a medium skillet over high heat, melt the butter. Add the mushrooms, green onions, and the remaining ½ teaspoon (2 mL) salt and sauté until the mushrooms are soft, 2 to 3 minutes. Mound the mushrooms in warmed bowls.

Pour the broth, with the herbs and pine needles, into a French press and slowly press the plunger down. (If you do not have a French press, strain through a fine-mesh sieve before using.) At the table, gently pour the broth around the mushrooms.

Tip For a clear broth, skim off any foam or fat when making stock. Do not boil the broth.

6 cups (1.5 L) Venison Stock (page 70) or chicken stock

2 big handfuls of green pine needles

6 sprigs fresh thyme

4 bay leaves

1 tablespoon (15 mL) black peppercorns

1 teaspoon (5 mL) kosher salt, divided

1 tablespoon (15 mL) unsalted butter

1 pound (450 g) wild mushrooms (such as pine, chanterelle, oyster, or trumpet), roughly chopped (about 2 cups/500 mL)

½ cup (125 mL) sliced green onion (white and light green parts only)

Foraging for mushrooms is one of my favourite things to do, and this salad is the best way to show off their distinctive flavours. You can use as many different types of mushrooms as you want or simply use your favourite ones. (For the salad in the photo I used boletes, Amanita jacksonii, and chanterelles.) I cut the mushrooms into similar sizes so they cook evenly all at the same time. I also recommend cooking the mushrooms at a very high heat to caramelize them and help seal in the flavourful moisture, rather than slowly cooking and rendering the liquid, which results in more of a stew-like appearance and taste.

WARM WILD MUSHROOM SALAD

Serves 4 as an appetizer

Heat a large skillet over high heat. Add 2 tablespoons (30 mL) of the olive oil. Add half of the mushrooms, half of the green onions, ½ teaspoon (2 mL) of the salt, and pepper to taste. Sauté until caramelized and tender, 2 to 3 minutes. Deglaze with 1 tablespoon (15 mL) of the sumac vinaigrette. Remove the mushroom mixture from the pan.

Return the pan to high heat, add the remaining 2 tablespoons (30 mL) olive oil, and sauté the remaining mushrooms and green onions, seasoning with the remaining ½ teaspoon (2 mL) salt and pepper to taste. Deglaze with the remaining 1 tablespoon (15 mL) sumac vinaigrette.

Divide the salad among plates or serve family-style in a large bowl. Scatter the fresh oregano, wood sorrel, and lemon balm on top.

4 tablespoons (60 mL) olive oil, divided
2 pounds (900 g) wild mushrooms, cut into 2-inch (5 cm) pieces, divided
1 bunch green onions (white parts only), thinly sliced, divided
1 teaspoon (5 mL) kosher salt, divided
Freshly cracked black pepper
2 tablespoons (30 mL) Sumac Vinaigrette (page 141), divided

GARNISH
Fresh oregano leaves
Fresh wood sorrel leaves
Fresh sliced lemon balm leaves

My earliest memory of puffball mushrooms was finding them when we were kids and throwing them at each other. I had no idea they were edible or so tasty. They can grow to massive sizes, sometimes 2 to 3 feet (60 to 90 cm) in diameter, but they need to be harvested quickly or they risk being infested by worms. Puffballs are best eaten when the inside is pure white; a yellow or brownish inside usually means they are past their prime and beginning to rot.

Puffballs can be found randomly growing in grassy fields throughout the summer and into early fall. They are delicious fried in butter or, as here, served cold as an appetizer. I would compare the flavour of these huge edibles to oyster mushrooms. When cooked the texture is similar to soft tofu, but when pressed into this carpaccio, the puffball has more of a firm texture much like a beef carpaccio. The nuts and cheese round out the dish with their rich flavour.

GIANT PUFFBALL CARPACCIO

Serves 4 to 6 as an appetizer

In a large stockpot, combine the water, white wine vinegar, sugar, salt, coriander seeds, chili flakes, garlic, cinnamon sticks, and bay leaves. Bring to a boil over high heat. Remove from the heat and carefully submerge the mushroom slices in the water, weighing them down with a dinner plate. Let the water cool to room temperature.

Using a slotted spoon, remove the mushroom slices and, using a rolling pin, press them between layers of paper towel. Squeeze out as much liquid as possible, changing the paper towel once or twice. Discard the soaking liquid.

Arrange the flattened pickled mushrooms on dinner plates. In a medium bowl, toss together the arugula, sumac vinaigrette, black pepper, and a pinch of salt. Garnish the mushrooms with the arugula salad, espelette pepper, walnuts, and Parmesan.

6 cups (1.5 L) water

4 cups (1 L) white wine vinegar

4 cups (1 L) granulated sugar

1 tablespoon (15 mL) kosher salt, more for seasoning

2 tablespoons (30 mL) coriander seeds

1 teaspoon (5 mL) red chili flakes

6 cloves garlic

2 cinnamon sticks

4 bay leaves

2 pounds (900 g) giant puffball mushrooms, outer skin peeled, sliced into rounds ½ inch (1 cm) thick

2 cups (500 mL) baby arugula

2 tablespoons (30 mL) Sumac Vinaigrette (page 141)

½ teaspoon (2 mL) black pepper

½ teaspoon (2 mL) espelette pepper

¼ cup (60 mL) chopped black walnuts

¼ cup (60 mL) freshly grated Parmesan cheese

One of the best ways to enjoy wild mushrooms is in an omelette. The earthiness of the mushrooms with the richness of eggs is a classic combination. At Antler we fill our mushroom omelettes with smoked fresh mozzarella and smoked cheddar.

The trick to making a perfect omelette is practice and a perfectly seasoned omelette pan or brand-new nonstick pan that you guard sacredly and never scrub and always store wrapped in a kitchen towel.

FORAGER'S OMELETTE

Serves 1

Heat a small skillet over high heat. Add 1 tablespoon (15 mL) of the butter and the mushrooms and sauté until softened, 2 to 3 minutes. Remove from the heat.

In a small bowl, whisk together the eggs, milk, 1 tablespoon (15 mL) of the olive oil, salt, and pepper.

Heat a large well-seasoned or nonstick skillet over medium-low heat. Add the remaining 1 tablespoon (15 mL) butter and 1 tablespoon (15 mL) olive oil, swirling to coat the pan. Pour the egg mixture into the pan, gently stirring with a spatula for 30 to 60 seconds. When the eggs start to coagulate on the bottom, stop stirring and let the eggs cook for 1 minute. Spoon the sautéed mushrooms down the middle of the omelette and top with the cheddar and mozzarella cheese. Fold the omelette in half or roll it. Garnish with sliced green onions and serve immediately.

2 tablespoons (30 mL) unsalted butter, divided

¼ pound (115 g) wild mushrooms (such as chanterelle, trumpet, morel, or oyster), washed, patted dry, and roughly chopped (about ½ cup/125 mL)

3 eggs

2 tablespoons (30 mL) whole milk

2 tablespoons (30 mL) olive oil, divided

½ teaspoon (2 mL) kosher salt

Freshly ground black pepper

⅓ cup (75 mL) grated smoked cheddar cheese

2 slices smoked mozzarella cheese (¼ inch/5 mm thick each)

Sliced green onion (white and light green parts only), for garnish

Everyone's favourite family breakfast meal, with homemade maple syrup and wild blueberry compote. Wild blueberries are in season during the summer months, and whenever I see them I'm reminded of picking them at my family cottage as a boy. It is probably one of my oldest memories of foraging. Wild blueberries are a perfect example of how the wild variety tastes far superior to the cultivated version. Wild berries are smaller, firmer in texture, a touch more acidic, and bursting with flavour.

WILD BLUEBERRY FRENCH TOAST

Serves 4 to 6

Make the Wild Blueberry Compote

In a medium saucepan, lightly crush the blueberries with a potato masher. Add the sugar and cinnamon stick and simmer until most of the liquid from the berries has been reduced and the compote appears thicker like a loose jam, 15 to 20 minutes. Stir in the lemon zest and juice. Discard the cinnamon stick. Store in an airtight container in the fridge for up to 1 week.

Make the French Toast

Preheat the oven to 325°F (160°C). Line a baking sheet with parchment paper.

In a large bowl, whisk together the eggs, cream, vanilla, cinnamon, and nutmeg.

Heat a large skillet over medium heat. Melt 1 tablespoon (15 mL) of the butter in the pan. Working in batches, dip the bread slices into the egg mixture, coating both sides. Let excess egg mixture drip back into the bowl. Fry the bread until golden brown, adding more butter as needed, 2 to 3 minutes per side. Transfer to the prepared baking sheet and keep warm in the oven while you cook the rest.

To serve, pour the maple syrup over the French toast, top with a scoop of blueberry compote, and dust with icing sugar.

WILD BLUEBERRY COMPOTE

2 cups (500 mL) wild blueberries
¾ cup (175 mL) granulated sugar
1 cinnamon stick
Zest and juice of 1 lemon

FRENCH TOAST

2 eggs
⅔ cup (150 mL) light (10%) cream
1 teaspoon (5 mL) vanilla paste or extract
1 teaspoon (5 mL) cinnamon
Pinch of nutmeg
4 tablespoons (60 mL) unsalted butter, for frying
6 thick slices of bread (I prefer whole wheat sourdough)
Pure maple syrup (I prefer the dark variety), for serving
1 tablespoon (15 mL) icing sugar, for dusting

I love fluffy pancakes! The trick to a fluffy texture is to separate the egg whites, whip them, and fold them into the batter. I use wild blueberries here, but you can use chocolate chips or strawberries or whatever you like. And of course, drown your pancakes in maple syrup, preferably local or homemade!

WILD BLUEBERRY PANCAKES

Serves 4

Preheat the oven to 200°F (100°C). Line a baking sheet with parchment paper.

In a large bowl, whisk together the flour, baking powder, baking soda, salt, and vanilla. Add the milk and egg yolks and whisk until smooth.

In a separate large bowl, whisk the egg whites vigorously to medium-stiff peaks. The whites should resemble whipped cream but be a bit frothier and looser. (If they look curdled or lumpy, they are overwhipped and you should start over with fresh egg whites.) Gently but thoroughly fold half of the egg whites into the batter. Fold in the remaining egg whites. The batter should look smooth and frothy.

Heat a large skillet over medium heat. Add 1 tablespoon (15 mL) of the butter to the pan. Pour about ⅓ cup (75 mL) of the batter per pancake into the hot pan, making a 3-inch (8 cm) circle. Sprinkle some blueberries on top of the pancakes and cook until the edges are golden brown and little air bubbles form on the surface, 2 to 3 minutes. Flip the pancakes and cook for another 1 to 2 minutes, adding more butter as needed. Transfer to the baking sheet and keep warm in the oven while you cook the remaining pancakes.

Stack the pancakes and serve with butter and maple syrup.

1¼ cups (300 mL) all-purpose flour

2 teaspoons (10 mL) baking powder

1 teaspoon (5 mL) baking soda

½ teaspoon (2 mL) kosher salt

1 teaspoon (5 mL) vanilla paste or extract

1 cup (250 mL) whole milk

3 eggs, separated

8 tablespoons (125 mL) unsalted butter, divided, for frying and serving

½ cup (125 mL) wild blueberries

Pure maple syrup (I prefer the dark variety), for serving

Chaga mushrooms do not look like mushrooms, and they are not the kind you can take a bite of. They are extremely woody and resemble a black knot growing externally on a tree trunk. Chaga are usually harvested by chipping them off the tree with an axe. They can be found growing on birch trees in the northern regions of North America, Europe, and Asia. Chaga has been used for centuries in Siberia and Asia as well as in Indigenous cultures as a healing medicine and herbal tea. Gaining popularity in the Western world, it is now readily available in health food stores and specialty tea shops, in chunks or ground in tea bags.

Chaga has a very mild, earthy flavour that lends itself nicely to chai spices. If you are using whole chaga mushrooms, you will need to break them into pieces with a hammer. Do not throw away the chaga; it can be used repeatedly until it stops colouring the water black.

CHAGA MUSHROOM TEA LATTE

Serves 6

In a large saucepan, combine the water, mushrooms, cinnamon sticks, ginger, cardamom, cloves, peppercorns, and maple syrup (if using). Simmer over low heat for 10 minutes; do not stir. The water will turn black. Strain the liquid, keeping the chaga for another use. The tea can be cooled, covered, and stored in the fridge for up to 1 week. Reheat before adding the steamed milk.

Steam the milk (if using) and fill mugs with half tea and half steamed milk.

6 cups (1.5 L) water

1 pound (450 g) chaga mushroom pieces

2 cinnamon sticks

1 piece (1 inch/2.5 cm) fresh ginger

1 tablespoon (15 mL) cardamom pods

1 tablespoon (15 mL) whole cloves

1 teaspoon (5 mL) black peppercorns

½ cup (125 mL) pure maple syrup (optional)

Whole milk, for steaming (optional)

This is my savoury take on the classic French dessert apple tarte Tatin. The rich, flaky pastry encrusts the sweet, creamy caramelized onions and earthy morels before the tart is inverted. Morels are my favourite in this dish, but any wild mushrooms can be substituted, such as chanterelles, oysters, shiitakes, or cremini. The wild leek pesto is a perfect tangy accompaniment, and the leeks and morels are in season at the same time.

MOREL MUSHROOM AND CARAMELIZED ONION TARTE TATIN

Makes 4 tartlets

Make the Quick Puff Pastry

Preheat the oven to 400°F (200°C).

In a large bowl, combine the flour and salt. Add the butter and, using your hands, crumble the butter cubes into the flour until three-quarters of the butter has been incorporated but you can still see some pea-size pieces. Add the water and mix until the dough just comes together. Turn out the dough onto a small baking sheet (6 ½ x 9 ½ inches/16 x 24 cm) lined with plastic wrap. Using your hands or a lightly floured rolling pin, flatten the dough into the pan about 1 inch (2.5 cm) thick, then wrap in plastic wrap. The dough should be in rectangular shape of the pan. Let rest for 10 minutes in the fridge.

Dust a work surface with flour. Transfer the dough to the work surface and dust with flour. Roll out the dough to ¼-inch (5 mm) thickness. Fold the dough into thirds, like you are folding a letter. Repeat rolling and folding two more times. This process creates the layers of butter and dough that cause the pastry to puff when baked. Roll out to ¼-inch (5 mm) thickness one final time and let rest for 5 minutes before cutting.

Using a 5-inch (12 cm) round cookie cutter, cut out 4 circles. Wrap any extra dough in plastic wrap and freeze for another use.

Assemble the Tarts

Arrange four 4-inch (10 cm) tartlet pans on a baking sheet and heat in the oven for 5 minutes. Evenly divide the butter and grapeseed oil among the pans. Add the mushrooms to cover the bottom of the pans. Season the mushrooms with a pinch of salt and pepper, thyme, and chili

QUICK PUFF PASTRY DOUGH

1¾ cups (425 mL/210 g) bread flour

½ teaspoon (2 mL) kosher salt

½ pound (225 g/1 cup/250 mL) cold unsalted butter, cut into cubes

⅓ cup (75 mL) cold water

FILLING

4 tablespoons (60 mL) unsalted butter

2 tablespoons (30 mL) grapeseed oil or vegetable oil

4 cups (1 L) cut in half lengthwise morel mushrooms, washed, patted dry, and trimmed

Pinch each of kosher salt and black pepper

2 teaspoons (10 mL) chopped fresh thyme

Pinch of red chili flakes

½ cup (125 mL) Caramelized Onions (page 65)

Garlic mustard leaves and flowers, for garnish

¼ cup (60 mL) Wild Leek Pesto (page 228)

flakes. Spread 2 tablespoons (30 mL) of the caramelized onions over each tart. Top with the pastry circles and gently press down to fit flush inside the tart pan.

Bake until the pastry is dark golden, 30 to 40 minutes. Carefully run a knife around the edge of the tart crust to separate it from the pan. Invert a heatproof plate over the tart and turn the pan upside down on the plate; carefully lift away the pan. With a spatula, remove any filling stuck to pan and arrange over the tart. Repeat to plate the remaining tarts. Garnish with garlic mustard leaves and flowers and wild leek pesto.

Rich, creamy, luscious risotto is the perfect vessel for your foraged mushrooms. Any mushroom or combination of your favourite mushrooms can be used. The traditional way to serve risotto is flat on a plate, as the flavour enhances as the risotto cools slightly.

For the Parmesan crisp garnish, you will need to freshly grate Parmesan from a wedge. Store-bought grated Parmesan will not work in this recipe.

WILD MUSHROOM RISOTTO

Serves 4 to 6

Preheat the oven to 400°F (200°C). Line a baking sheet with parchment paper.

Evenly sprinkle ½ cup (125 mL) of the Parmesan on the prepared baking sheet. You want a very thin layer of cheese. Bake for 6 to 8 minutes or until golden brown and crispy. Let cool. Break into pieces and set aside.

In a medium saucepan over medium heat, heat the vegetable stock.

In another medium saucepan over medium heat, melt the butter. Add the rice and toast the rice in the butter, stirring constantly, for 2 minutes. Add the mushrooms, shallots, garlic, thyme, salt, and pepper and continue cooking, stirring, for 2 more minutes. Add the wine and 1 cup (250 mL) of the hot stock and cook, stirring occasionally, until most of the liquid has been absorbed. Continue ladling stock into the rice, 1 cup (250 mL) at a time, and stirring until the liquid is absorbed before adding more, until the rice is a thick but loose porridge-like consistency, 15 to 20 minutes. Remove from the heat and stir in the mascarpone cheese and remaining ½ cup (125 mL) Parmesan. Adjust seasoning, if needed.

Spoon the risotto onto plates, arrange the Parmesan crisps on top, and serve immediately.

1 cup (250 mL) freshly grated Parmesan cheese, divided

4 cups (1 L) vegetable or light chicken stock (see page 70)

¼ cup (60 mL) unsalted butter

1½ cups (375 mL) Arborio rice

1 pound (450 g) wild yellow foot chanterelle mushrooms, roughly chopped (about 2 cups/500 mL)

½ cup (125 mL) minced shallot

2 tablespoons (30 mL) minced garlic

1 teaspoon (5 mL) chopped fresh thyme

1 teaspoon (5 mL) kosher salt

½ teaspoon (2 mL) freshly ground black pepper

½ cup (125 mL) dry white wine

2 tablespoons (30 mL) mascarpone cheese

You can harvest just the greens of wild leeks (ramps) without uprooting the bulb; this ensures the survival of the plant. The greens can be sautéed like spinach or made into this pesto to add to pastas or fish or meat dishes. I like to serve this pesto on top of the Morel Mushroom and Caramelized Onion Tarte Tatin (page 224). Do not add the salt until just before serving or the pesto will turn brown.

WILD LEEK PESTO

Makes 3 cups (750 mL)

In a food processor, combine the wild leek greens, walnuts, Parmesan, garlic, pepper, and chili flakes. With the processor running, slowly pour the olive oil through the feed tube and blend until emulsified. Store the pesto (without the salt) in an airtight container in the fridge for 2 to 3 days. Add the salt just before serving.

Variations

MARSH MARIGOLD PESTO

Marsh marigold is one of the first indicators of spring. It grows in every province in Canada and over half of the United States in wet marshes, swamps, and moist soil (hence its name). If you are a lover of bitter greens such as rapini and dandelion, this one is for you. The leaves can be sautéed and used in any dish where you would use cooked greens. Blanching the plant is a must. It cannot be eaten raw because it contains a natural toxin that is killed by heat. Marsh marigold flower buds can be pickled and used just like capers.

Use the basic recipe above to make marsh marigold pesto, replacing the wild leeks with the same quantity of blanched marsh marigold greens.

2 cups (500 mL) wild leek greens
½ cup (125 mL) raw walnuts
¼ cup (60 mL) freshly grated Parmesan cheese
1 teaspoon (5 mL) minced garlic
½ teaspoon (2 mL) freshly ground black pepper
½ teaspoon (2 mL) red chili flakes
½ cup (125 mL) olive oil
1 teaspoon (5 mL) kosher salt

GARLIC MUSTARD PESTO

Garlic mustard is a tasty herb with hints of garlic and mustard, just as its name suggests. It is also one of North America's most invasive plants. Originally brought over from Europe as a culinary herb, it has escaped into the wild and is choking out native wildflowers and blanketing forest floors. Garlic mustard is a great addition to salads, makes a delicious pesto, and can be sautéed just like spinach.

Use the basic recipe above to make garlic mustard pesto, replacing the wild leeks with the same quantity of garlic mustard.

The spring season for wild leeks, or ramps, is very short—just a few weeks to a month at the most. I love to pickle the bulbs so I can enjoy them all year long. They rival any pickle sliced and served in a sandwich, on a charcuterie board, or with a nice tartare. This recipes uses the bulbs only. The green part of the leek can be sautéed or made into pesto (page 228).

PICKLED WILD LEEKS

Makes 2 quarts (2 L)

In a medium pot, combine all the ingredients and bring to a boil over high heat. Divide between two 1-quart (1 L) sterilized mason jars. Seal with a lid while hot and let cool to room temperature. Store, unopened, in the fridge for up to 1 year. Once opened, store in the fridge for several months. To store the jars in a cold cellar, follow proper canning procedures for your canning device.

4 cups (1 L) wild leek bulbs (white part only)

1½ cups (375 mL) water

1¼ cups (300 mL) white wine vinegar

1¼ cups (300 mL) granulated sugar

2 cinnamon sticks

1 tablespoon (15 mL) whole cloves

1 tablespoon (15 mL) mustard seeds

1 tablespoon (15 mL) coriander seeds

A family friend gave me saffron milk cap mushrooms and this pickling recipe. From August to late fall, saffron caps start popping up in the coniferous forests. Bright orange in colour, they are high in beta-carotene and typically grow in abundance, making them fun and easy to pick. These mushroom have a great firm texture and fragrant flavour that makes a great preserve.

PICKLED SAFFRON MILK CAP MUSHROOMS

Makes 2 quarts (2 L)

In a medium pot, combine all the ingredients. Simmer over medium heat for 20 minutes. Divide between two 1-quart (1 L) sterilized mason jars. Seal while hot and let cool to room temperature. Store, unopened, in the fridge for up to 1 year. Once opened, store in the fridge for up to 6 months. To store the jars in a cold cellar, follow proper canning procedures for your canning device.

2 pounds (900 g) saffron milk cap mushrooms, brushed clean (about 4 cups/1 L)
1 cup (250 mL) diced white onion
1⅔ cups (400 mL) granulated sugar
1¼ cups (300 mL) water
½ cup (125 mL) white vinegar
½ cup (125 mL) white wine vinegar
5 whole cloves
1 small cinnamon stick
Pinch of nutmeg

These mushrooms are one of the easiest and safest for a beginner forager to look for as they do not have any poisonous lookalikes. Its formal name is dryad's saddle, but it is commonly called pheasant back or hawk's wing for its feathery appearance. These mushrooms grow in abundance most of the year, but they are most tender in the spring when they first sprout. I find that when they're over 6 inches (15 cm) in diameter they are too tough and woody.

Pheasant backs have a very floral, sweet smell of green watermelon rind. Meaty in texture, they are perfectly suited for pickling and preserving. A similar mushroom in texture is the king oyster, but flavour-wise there is no substitute.

PICKLED PHEASANT BACK MUSHROOMS

Makes 2 quarts (2 L)

In a medium pot, combine all the ingredients. Bring to a boil over high heat and boil for 3 minutes. Divide among sterilized jars. Seal while hot and let cool to room temperature. Store, unopened, in the fridge for up to 1 year. Once opened, store in the fridge for several months. To store the jars in a cold cellar, follow proper canning procedures for your canning device.

2 pounds (900 g) pheasant back mushrooms, washed, dried, and sliced (about 4 cups/1 L)

1½ cups (375 mL) water

1 cup (250 mL) white wine vinegar

1 cup (250 mL) granulated sugar

2 cinnamon sticks

1 tablespoon (15 mL) whole cloves

1 tablespoon (15 mL) mustard seeds

1 tablespoon (15 mL) coriander seeds

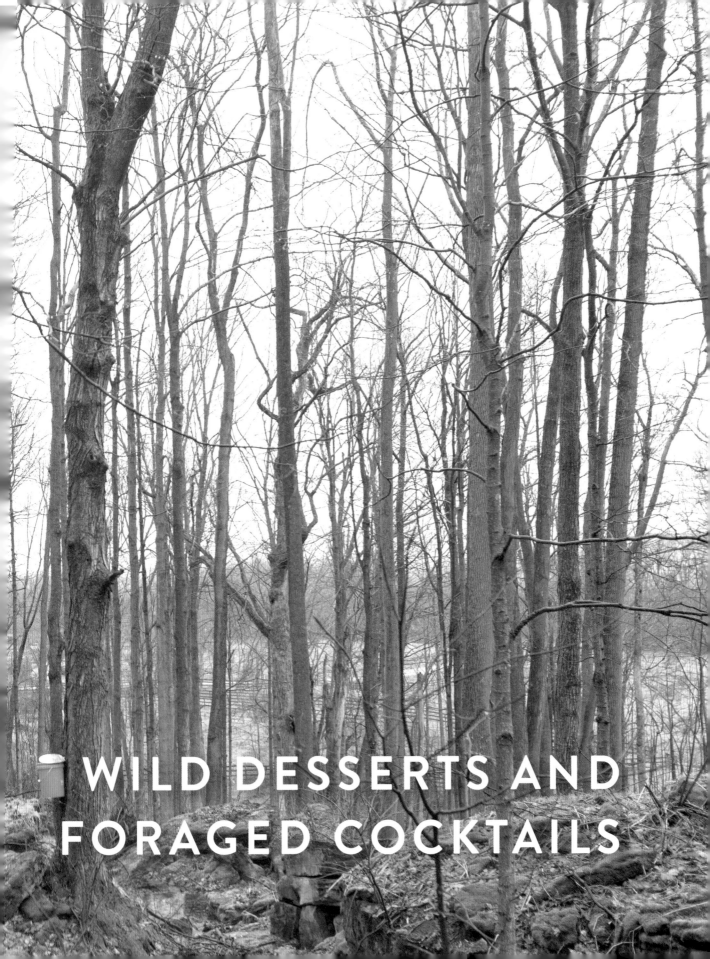

WILD DESSERTS AND FORAGED COCKTAILS

SPRING THAW

MAPLE SYRUP SEASON IS MY favourite time of year. The maple run is my first wild experience that happens after the deep freeze of winter. As the daytime temperatures rise, then drop back to freezing at night, that's when the sap runs best. The sugar maples are sucking water from the earth to feed their buds while the rest of us are just starting to imagine spring. It takes me back to those school field trips to the sugar shack. I loved watching the hot syrup hit the fresh snow and then rolling it up on a Popsicle stick before it could harden.

Maple syrup is Canada's national natural sweetener. It's what goes into our cocktails and desserts. In fact, we tap sap at a friend's country acreage and then reduce it in the Antler kitchen. That's when you appreciate how precious it is. It takes eighteen litres of sap to get one litre of maple syrup.

Maple is just the start. We have a lot of fun tapping all kinds of exotic flavours. Many of them can be found in any city park. And many of the techniques are as old as time. The First Nations have been tapping maple and making tea from conifers for thousands of years.

At Antler we take cedar boughs and boil them with sugar and water, then pour the liquid into an ice-cream machine to create an amazing cedar ice. Or we dry the cedar, grind it, and then sprinkle it over ice cream. We do the same with pine needles, sumac, and spruce. There are so many natural ingredients just outside our back door, including wild ginger. It's not the same family as regular ginger but it's every bit as flavourful, a little spicier and more floral. It, too, makes an amazing ice cream. And we use local rosehip as an infuser for dessert and pastry creams. Rosehip is a bit like ice wine; the colder it gets, the sweeter the flavour. You cannot get more Canadian than that!

These local flavours are not just for dessert. Our cocktail menu, from wild mint mojito to wild blackberry lemonade, is a tribute to our extensive and intensive recipe testing. We make our own bitters infused with sumac or black walnut. And we tap local distillers, brewers, and vintners. One of my favourite cocktails features an exquisite wild-caught prawn from the British Columbia coast. Perched on a glass rimmed with celery salt and cedar ash, the Spot Prawn Caesar (page 268) is the perfect start to an Antler brunch.

Maple syrup is quite easy to harvest. A quick internet search and some simple tools will get you started with a minimal investment. You will need a drill, taps or spiles, a few buckets with lids, a huge stockpot for reducing, and at least one maple tree—preferably a sugar maple. A sugar maple produces sap with double the sugar content of its relatives the red maple, silver maple, and black maple. Look for a maple tree that has bright pink leaves in the fall when the colours change and shaggy silvery-looking bark. Mark that tree and then wait until spring.

The maple season is controlled by the weather. You can start collecting sap in the spring once the temperature goes above zero in the day but is still below freezing at night. At this time the tree is desperately sucking up water to feed its branches to make their new leaves. Once the weather consistently stays above freezing, the sap will stop running. Sometimes the season is only a couple of weeks long, but in a good season the sap can run for a month or so.

Maple sap straight from the tree is great for your health. It's full of electrolytes and minerals—much like coconut water but without the carbon footprint of shipping.

Once you have a full bucket of sap, it is time to reduce it. An outdoor burner is ideal, but you can reduce indoors as long as you have an exhaust fan and crack a window. Reduce the maple syrup rapidly over high heat in a stockpot until the temperature hits 219°F to 220°F (103°C to 104°C). Then pour your very own pure maple syrup into sterilized jars and seal. Store in the fridge or follow proper canning procedures and store in a cool pantry or cellar.

When I think of fudge, general stores in rural towns where I grew up come to mind. In today's world of giant corporate chocolate and candy companies, fudge is not as common to find, but this recipe will take you back to that time you ate it as a kid. This fudge is rich, creamy, and decadent, with the perfect amount of maple flavour. It can be enjoyed on its own or shaved over ice cream or on top of Maple Bacon Doughnuts (page 252).

MAPLE FUDGE

Makes 10 pieces

Line a 9- × 5-inch (2 L) loaf pan with plastic wrap.

In a large pot over medium heat, melt the butter. Add the brown sugar, evaporated milk, and maple syrup. Bring to a boil over medium-high heat, stirring, and boil until thick, about 12 minutes. Remove from the heat and whisk in the icing sugar. Transfer the mixture to the bowl of a stand mixer fitted with the paddle attachment and mix on medium speed for 5 minutes. The fudge will have cooled slightly and have a firm, doughy texture.

Scrape the fudge into the prepared pan. Using a rubber spatula, press the fudge firmly into the pan and smooth and flatten the top. Cover with plastic wrap and let set in the fridge for about 4 hours. Once chilled, cut into 1-inch (2.5 cm) pieces. Store tightly wrapped at room temperature.

1 pound (450 g/2 cups/500 mL) unsalted butter

1 bag (2.2 pounds/1 kg) brown sugar

1 cup (250 mL) evaporated milk

½ cup (125 mL) pure maple syrup

1 bag (2.2 pounds/1 kg) icing sugar

This is one of my favourite desserts, with a flavour much like a butter tart. Maple sugar pie originated in Quebec, where it is called tarte au sucre. You can also make it as six small tarts. Serve topped with whipped cream.

MAPLE SUGAR PIE

Makes 1 large pie or 6 small tarts

Preheat the oven to 350°F (180°C).

On a lightly floured work surface, roll out the dough into a 12-inch (30 cm) circle. Loosely roll the dough over the rolling pin and transfer the pastry to a 9-inch (23 cm) pie plate. Gently press the dough into the pan and trim the edges flush with the pan. Wrap any extra dough in plastic wrap and freeze for another use.

In a large bowl, whisk together the eggs, maple syrup, condensed milk, brown sugar, Calvados, salt, and cinnamon (if using). Pour the filling into the pie shell and bake until the centre is set but jiggles like jelly, 45 to 50 minutes. (If you are baking smaller tarts, bake for 30 to 35 minutes.) Let the pie cool on a rack for at least 30 minutes before slicing.

Serve slices of pie or individual tarts topped with whipped cream and candied walnuts (if using).

1 batch of Butter Pastry Dough (page 59) or store-bought
4 large eggs
2 cups (500 mL) pure maple syrup
1½ cups (375 mL) sweetened condensed milk (or evaporated milk for a less sweet option)
1 cup (250 mL) packed brown sugar
2 tablespoons (30 mL) Calvados or brandy
Pinch of kosher salt
Pinch of cinnamon (optional)

FOR SERVING
Whipped cream
Chopped candied walnuts (optional)

Antler is located in the Little Portugal neighbourhood of Toronto. If you know anything about Portuguese desserts, pastel de nata is sure to be one of your favourites. The flaky pastry is filled with a sweet custard and served warm—it's heavenly. When the restaurant was under construction, we got to know our neighbouring bakers quite well for their addictive egg tarts. Naturally, I had to learn to make them and put our maple syrup twist on it.

MAPLE CUSTARD TARTS

Makes 20 mini tarts

On a lightly floured surface, roll out the puff pastry dough until it is about ⅛-inch (3 mm) thick. Using a knife, trim the dough into a 10-inch (25 cm) square. It does not have to be an exact square. Spread the butter in a thin layer over the dough, then tightly roll the dough into a log, wrap in plastic wrap, and chill in the fridge for at least 3 hours.

Preheat the oven to 500°F (260°C).

Remove the dough log from the fridge, discard the plastic wrap, and cut twenty ½-inch (1 cm) thick discs. Press the dough discs into 20 cups of a mini muffin tin, pressing the dough up the sides like you would with a crumble type of crust for pie. Chill until firm, at least 10 minutes.

In a medium saucepan over high heat, bring half of the milk, the water, and sugar to a boil; boil until the sugar is dissolved, 3 to 4 minutes. Remove from the heat.

In a medium bowl, whisk together the remaining milk and the flour. While whisking, add the hot milk mixture and the maple syrup, whisking until smooth. Return to the saucepan and cook over medium heat, stirring constantly, until the mixture begins to thicken, 2 to 3 minutes. Remove from the heat.

In a separate medium bowl, whisk the egg yolks. While whisking, slowly add the hot milk mixture. Strain the mixture through a fine-mesh sieve to remove any little membranes from the egg whites. It should resemble thick heavy cream. Divide the filling among the tart shells and fill just below the top.

Bake until the pastry is dark golden brown and the custard has dark caramelized spots, 15 to 20 minutes. Let cool on a rack for 5 minutes before removing the tarts from the tin. The tarts are best served warm or at room temperature the same day. Store in an airtight container in the fridge for up to 2 days.

1 batch of Quick Puff Pastry Dough (page 224)
½ cup (125 mL) unsalted butter, at room temperature
3¼ cups (800 mL) whole milk, divided
1½ cups (375 mL) water
1 cup (250 mL) granulated sugar
1 cup (250 mL) all-purpose flour
1 cup (250 mL) pure maple syrup
12 large egg yolks

This classic dessert's sweet, crispy top is a great contrast to the rich, creamy custard underneath. The fun part is carmelizing the top with a kitchen torch. You can use your oven broiler, but you risk overheating your custard, and anyway, you miss all the fun. So buy an inexpensive kitchen torch for ten to twenty dollars—you will not regret it. It's a great tool to have around the house. (It's my secret trick for lighting my charcoal barbecue quickly.)

I make my custard with granulated maple sugar, but make sure you use granulated white sugar for the caramelized top. Maple sugar will not caramelize when torched—it catches fire. Slowly whisking the hot cream into the egg yolks is called tempering. If you add all the cream at once, you risk scrambling the yolks, resulting in an unpleasant taste and curdled texture.

MAPLE CRÈME BRÛLÉE

Serves 6

Preheat the oven to 330°F (165°C).

In a medium saucepan, combine the cream, maple sugar, vanilla, and salt. Heat over high heat until scalding (almost simmering), whisking briefly to dissolve the sugar.

In a large bowl, whisk the egg yolks. While whisking, slowly add ½ cup (125 mL) of the hot cream mixture, then pour in the remaining cream, whisking constantly. Strain the mixture through a fine-mesh sieve to remove any little membranes from the egg whites. Divide the mixture among six 5-ounce (150 mL) ramekins.

Using a kitchen torch, quickly torch the top of the custards to burst any bubbles. Place the ramekins in a casserole dish and add enough hot water to come halfway up the sides of the ramekins. Cover the casserole dish with foil. Bake until custard resembles jelly when jiggled, 30 to 45 minutes. Overbaked custard will be curdled. Using tongs, remove the custards from the water and cool in the fridge for at least 4 hours before serving.

When ready to serve, evenly sprinkle 1 tablespoon (15 mL) white sugar on top of each custard. Torch the top, moving the flame back and forth, until the sugar caramelizes and liquefies, carefully tilting the ramekin so the liquid caramel evenly coats the top. Serve immediately.

4 cups (1 L) heavy (35%) cream
½ cup (125 mL) granulated maple sugar
1 teaspoon (5 mL) vanilla paste or extract
Pinch of kosher salt
6 large egg yolks
6 tablespoons (90 mL) granulated white sugar, for torching

This is a nod to my English heritage. Sticky toffee pudding is an English classic that provides warmth and comfort during the bleak months of winter. The pudding is essentially a steamed cake, resulting in a soft, rich texture. Paired with salted maple caramel is incredible. And the maple makes it fitting for the Canadian winter!

STICKY TOFFEE PUDDING WITH SALTED MAPLE CARAMEL

Serves 6 to 8

Preheat the oven to 330°F (165°C). Butter a 9- × 5-inch (2 L) loaf pan.

Make the Sticky Toffee Pudding

In a medium bowl, cover the dates with the boiling water. Let soak for 5 minutes.

In a large bowl with an electric mixer, or stand mixer fitted with the paddle attachment, beat the butter with the brown sugar until well mixed and fluffy. Add the eggs and beat until incorporated. Add the dates with their soaking liquid and mix on low speed until fully combined, about 1 minute. Add the flour, baking powder, baking soda, cinnamon, nutmeg, and salt and mix on low speed to combine, about 3 minutes. Pour the batter into the prepared loaf pan.

Place the loaf pan in a deep casserole dish and add enough hot water to come halfway up the side of the loaf pan. Cover with foil. Bake for 1 to 1½ hours, until the cake has risen and a wooden skewer poked in the middle comes out clean. If there is batter on the skewer, bake for another 15 to 20 minutes and check again.

Make the Salted Maple Caramel Sauce

In a small saucepan, combine the granulated sugar, corn syrup, and water. Boil over high heat, without stirring or shaking the pan, until the sugar caramelizes, 3 to 5 minutes. When the sugar is dark brown, whisk in the cream, butter, maple syrup, bourbon, and salt. Continue to cook until the caramel is smooth and thick, 3 to 5 minutes. Remove from the heat and keep warm.

To serve, pour salted maple caramel sauce over a slice of sticky toffee pudding. Top with a spoonful of whipped cream and a pinch of flaky sea salt.

STICKY TOFFEE PUDDING

2 cups (500 mL) chopped pitted dates
1⅔ cups (400 mL) boiling water
½ cup (125 mL) unsalted butter
1⅓ cups (325 mL) packed brown sugar
2 eggs
1⅓ cups (325 mL/160 g) all-purpose flour
2 teaspoons (10 mL) baking powder
1 teaspoon (5 mL) baking soda
1 teaspoon (5 mL) cinnamon
½ teaspoon (2 mL) nutmeg
Pinch of kosher salt

SALTED MAPLE CARAMEL SAUCE

½ cup (125 mL) granulated sugar
2 tablespoons (30 mL) corn syrup
2 tablespoons (30 mL) water
1 cup (250 mL) heavy (35%) cream
¾ cup (175 mL) unsalted butter
½ cup (125 mL) pure maple syrup
2 tablespoons (30 mL) bourbon
1 teaspoon (5 mL) sea salt

FOR SERVING

Whipped cream
Flaky sea salt

Eating a warm, freshly made doughnut will convert you from store-bought doughnuts forever. These are also fun for the kids to help make. These doughnuts are a rich and decadent treat. For an added bonus, serve them with Wild Ginger Ice Cream (page 261).

If you want to skip the bacon, in its place add 2½ tablespoons (37 mL) of butter to the glaze instead.

MAPLE BACON DOUGHNUTS

Makes 8 to 10 doughnuts

Make the Doughnuts

In a large bowl, stir together the warm water and yeast and let sit for 3 minutes. The yeast should start to foam. Add the eggs, milk, duck fat, granulated sugar, and salt. Whisk to combine.

In the bowl of a stand mixer fitted with the dough hook, combine the flour and yeast mixture and mix on low speed for 8 to 10 minutes, until the dough is smooth and no longer sticks to the sides of the bowl. Scrape the dough out onto a work surface and knead into a smooth ball. Place the dough ball in an oiled bowl, cover, and let rise until doubled in size, about 1 hour.

Grease a baking sheet with vegetable oil or cooking spray.

Transfer the dough to a lightly floured surface. Using a rolling pin, gently roll out to ½-inch (1 cm) thickness. Cut out 8 to 10 circles using a 3-inch (8 cm) round cookie or doughnut cutter. If you are using a cookie cutter you can poke a hole in the centre using your fingers and stretch the dough into a doughnut shape. Place the doughnuts on the prepared baking sheet. Place the baking sheet inside a large plastic bag, and let rise until doubled in size, about 1 hour.

While the doughnuts are rising, prepare the glaze and heat the oil in a large pot to 350°F (180°C) for deep-frying.

Make the Glaze

In a medium saucepan over medium heat, cook the bacon until it is beginning to brown and crisp, 3 to 5 minutes. Reduce the heat to low and whisk in the icing sugar, maple syrup, and vanilla. Adjust the consistency of the glaze with the hot water, adding 1 tablespoon (15 mL) at a time, as needed. The glaze should be loose but not watery. Keep warm.

DOUGHNUTS

½ cup (125 mL) warm water

2 packets (¼ ounce/7 g each) active dry yeast

2 large eggs

1⅓ cups (325 mL) warm whole milk

⅓ cup (75 mL) duck fat, lard, or shortening

½ cup (125 mL) granulated sugar

1 teaspoon (5 mL) kosher salt

4½ cups (1.125 L/540 g) all-purpose flour

8 cups (2 L) vegetable oil, for frying

GLAZE

1 cup (250 mL) diced bacon

2 cups (500 mL) icing sugar

¼ cup (60 mL) pure maple syrup

1 teaspoon (5 mL) pure vanilla extract

2 tablespoons (30 mL) hot water, as needed for desired consistency

Deep-Fry the Doughnuts

Once the doughnuts have doubled in size, working in batches, gently transfer them to the hot oil using your hands and a flat spatula or flipper. Fry until they are golden brown on both sides, about 2 minutes per side. Transfer to a rack set inside a baking sheet to drain. Dip the doughnuts in the glaze while they are still warm and place on the rack to cool slightly before serving

Spruce tastes a lot like pine and fir, with a slight hint of citrus. Spruce tips are high in vitamin C. They can be harvested in the spring when they are soft and supple. Once summer comes, the needles harden. They can still be consumed, but they'll have a more distinct flavour and harder texture, more suitable for infusions or for drying and blending into a powder. Unlike the classic heavy New York style cheesecake, this one is light and fluffy with a forest lemony hint of spruce.

SPRUCE TIP RICOTTA CHEESECAKE

Serves 6 to 8

Make the Crust

Preheat the oven to 350°F (180°C). Butter a 9-inch (2.5 L) springform pan. Tightly wrap the pan with foil to prevent water seeping in.

In a food processor, combine the butter, flour, oats, brown sugar, and walnuts. Pulse until combined but still crumbly in appearance with visible chunks of nuts. Press the crumb mixture firmly into the bottom of the springform pan. Wipe the bowl clean.

Make the Filling

In the food processor, combine all the filling ingredients. Process until smooth. Pour the filling over the crust and transfer to a baking dish. Fill the dish with enough hot water to come halfway up the side of the springform pan. Cover the baking dish with foil.

Bake until the cheesecake filling jiggles but is not runny, about 1¼ hours. Remove from the oven and let cool completely in the water. Remove the pan from the water, cover, and refrigerate for at least 4 hours before slicing.

To serve, run a thin knife around the edge before releasing the sides of the springform pan. Serve the cheesecake with blackberries overtop.

CRUST

½ cup (125 mL) unsalted butter, at room temperature, more for greasing the pan
½ cup (125 mL) all-purpose flour
½ cup (125 mL) old-fashioned rolled oats
½ cup (125 mL) packed brown sugar
½ cup (125 mL) black walnut halves

FILLING

5 eggs
1½ cups (375 mL) sour cream
1 cup (250 mL) mascarpone cheese
1 cup (250 mL) ricotta cheese
½ cup (125 mL) cream cheese
½ cup (125 mL) pure maple syrup
2 tablespoons (30 mL) minced fresh spruce tips (or 1 tablespoon/15 mL dried needles)
1 teaspoon (5 mL) vanilla paste or extract
½ teaspoon (2 mL) kosher salt

Blackberries, for garnish

Pumpkin pie is one of my favourite desserts. Nothing says "fall baking" like this pie. Naturally I sweeten my pie with granulated maple sugar and season it with aromatic spices for a richer depth of flavour.

If you choose to make the pumpkin purée yourself, look for the small sugar pumpkin variety in the grocery store. They are superior in flavour to the huge Halloween pumpkins.

SPICED PUMPKIN PIE

Serves 6

Preheat the oven to 425°F (220°C).

On a lightly floured work surface, roll out the dough into a 12-inch (30 cm) circle about ⅛-inch (3 mm) thick. Loosely roll the dough over the rolling pin and transfer the pastry to a 9-inch (23 cm) pie plate. Gently press the dough into the pan and trim the edges flush with the pan and crimp if desired. Wrap any extra dough in plastic wrap and freeze for another use.

In a food processor, combine all the filling ingredients. Process until smooth, 1 to 2 minutes. Pour the filling into the pie shell and place in the oven. Reduce the heat to 350°F (180°C) and bake for 30 to 45 minutes, until the centre of the pie is just set. A skewer inserted in the centre should come out clean. Transfer to a rack and let cool.

Make the Vanilla Whipped Cream

In a medium bowl, whisk together the cream, sugar, and vanilla until stiff peaks form.

Slice the pie and serve topped with vanilla whipped cream.

1 batch of Butter Pastry Dough (page 59)
1¾ cups (425 mL) pumpkin purée (about 1 small roasted sugar pumpkin)
1 cup (250 mL) granulated maple sugar
1 cup (250 mL) heavy (35%) cream
2 eggs
1 tablespoon (15 mL) grated fresh ginger (or ½ teaspoon/2 mL ground ginger)
1 tablespoon (15 mL) cinnamon
1 teaspoon (5 mL) vanilla paste or extract
½ teaspoon (2 mL) ground allspice
½ teaspoon (2 mL) ground cloves
½ teaspoon (2 mL) ground cardamom
¼ teaspoon (1 mL) freshly grated nutmeg
½ teaspoon (2 mL) kosher salt

VANILLA WHIPPED CREAM

½ cup (125 mL) heavy (35%) cream
1 teaspoon (5 mL) granulated sugar
½ teaspoon (2 mL) vanilla paste or extract

Summer is a busy time for picking ripe wild blueberries, blackberries, and raspberries. I remember spending hours as a kid filling buckets in the woods at the family cottage. We would always make this tart with whatever berries we found. Feel free to mix and match the types of berries and combinations you like.

Rather than making one big tart, you can make individual tarts (pictured using 4½-inch/11 cm square moulds). Decrease the cooking time 5 to 10 minutes for smaller tarts.

WILD BERRY TART

Serves 6 to 8

Preheat the oven to 400°F (200°C).

On a lightly floured work surface, roll out the dough into a 12-inch (30 cm) circle. Loosely roll the dough over the rolling pin and transfer the pastry to a 9-inch (23 cm) pie plate. Gently press the dough into the pan and trim the edges flush with the pan.

In large bowl, lightly crush the wild berries using the back of a wooden spoon or a potato masher. Add the sugar, flour, lemon juice, cinnamon, nutmeg, and salt. Gently mix until the flour is incorporated. Pour the berry mixture into the pie shell.

Bake until the crust is golden brown and the filling is bubbling, 35 to 45 minutes. Let cool on a rack before slicing. Garnish with sliced almonds and a dusting of icing sugar.

1 batch of Butter Pastry Dough (page 59)

3½ cups (875 mL) wild berries (such as blueberries, raspberries, or blackberries)

¾ cup (175 mL) granulated sugar

2 tablespoons (30 mL) all-purpose flour

1 teaspoon (5 mL) fresh lemon juice

½ teaspoon (2 mL) cinnamon

Pinch of nutmeg

Pinch of kosher salt

GARNISH

Sliced toasted almonds

Icing sugar, for dusting

Wild ginger is not part of the ginger family, but it has a very similar flavour with a floral note and spicy heat. Native to much of North America, it is easily found in forests during the spring and summer months. Wild ginger has an interconnected root system, so it is important to pick no more than 10 percent of a patch to ensure it will grow back. The roots are the flavourful part that you keep.

Wild ginger's floral taste and spice pair perfectly with the sweetness and creaminess of the caramelized apple in this tart. Choose your favourite apples for this dessert. I like Honeycrisp or Mutsu because of their flavour and firm texture, but a tart green Granny Smith will work as well.

APPLE TARTE TATIN WITH WILD GINGER ICE CREAM

Makes 4 individual tarts

Make the Wild Ginger Ice Cream

In a small saucepan, combine the cream, milk, vanilla, wild ginger, and half of the sugar. Heat, stirring to dissolve the sugar, until just about boiling and small bubbles are forming around the edge. Remove from the heat before the scald turns into a boil.

In a medium bowl, whisk together the egg yolks and the remaining half of the sugar until thick and pale. While whisking, slowly pour 1 cup (250 mL) of the hot cream mixture into the egg mixture. Slowly pour in the remaining cream mixture, whisking until incorporated. Leave the wild ginger roots in the custard, cover, and chill for at least 8 hours or overnight. You want the custard to be ice cold before churning.

Strain the mixture and discard the ginger. Pour the mixture into an ice-cream machine and churn according to the manufacturer's instructions until the ice cream looks thickened and frozen, up to 20 minutes depending on your machine. Scrape the ice cream into an airtight container and freeze until firm, about 2 hours. The ice cream will keep in the freezer for up to 1 week. After a week, I tend to notice freezer burn, which you want to avoid.

Make the Apple Tarte Tatin

Preheat the oven to 425°F (220°C).

On a lightly floured work surface, roll out the dough to ¼-inch (5 mm) thickness. Cut out 4 discs with a 4½-inch (11 cm) round cutter.

WILD GINGER ICE CREAM

1 cup (250 mL) heavy (35%) cream

1 cup (250 mL) whole milk

1 teaspoon (5 mL) pure vanilla extract or paste

½ pound (225 g) wild ginger root, washed and chopped, or sliced fresh ginger (skin on for added flavour)

¾ cup (175 mL) granulated sugar, divided

5 egg yolks

APPLE TARTE TATIN

1 batch of Quick Puff Pastry Dough (page 224)

4 tablespoons (60 mL) unsalted butter

4 tablespoons (60 mL) granulated sugar

4 green apples, peeled, cored, and sliced into ½-inch (1 cm) wedges

1 apple, peeled, cored, and thinly sliced, for garnish

recipe and ingredients continues

Place four 4½-inch (11 cm) tart pans on a baking sheet. Add 1 tablespoon (15 mL) butter to each pan and heat in the oven until melted. Evenly sprinkle 1 tablespoon (15 mL) sugar in each pan, then arrange the apple wedges in a circle or fan in each pan. Top each tart with a dough circle and tuck in the edges.

Put the tarts in the oven, reduce the oven temperature to 375°F (190°C), and bake for 35 to 45 minutes. The pastry should rise quite significantly and be dark golden, and the sugar and apples will be dark and caramelized. Invert the tarts onto plates. Garnish with fresh apple slices and top with a scoop of wild ginger ice cream.

This dessert is my take on a refined s'more. I replace store-bought marshmallow with fresh whipped meringue, make a rich chocolate mousse instead of hard chocolate, and replace the graham cracker with crisp Florentine cookies. At Antler, we use a smoke gun and a glass cloche to infuse the smoke flavour and reveal the smoke cloud at the table. At home, you can easily smoke the ingredients before making the dessert, in a smoker or using your kitchen torch. If you do not have a smoker, simply skip the smoking step and melt the chocolate with the cream in the microwave. The mousse will still be delicious. Crisp Florentine cookies are paper thin, almost like thin taffy.

SMOKED CHOCOLATE MOUSSE WITH FLORENTINE COOKIES

Serves 4 to 6

Make the Florentine Cookie Dough

In a small saucepan, melt the butter over medium heat. Add the sugar, corn syrup, cream, and walnuts. Bring to a boil and cook, without stirring, until the mixture thickens, 2 to 3 minutes. Pour into a wide container or bowl and cool, uncovered, in the fridge until the batter is firm, about 1 hour.

Make the Smoked Chocolate Mousse

Set the smoker to 250°F (125°C). In a medium stainless steel or glass bowl, combine the chocolate and 1 cup (250 mL) of the cream. Place the bowl in the smoker. Stir after 15 minutes. If there are still lumps, continue smoking for 5 minutes and check again. When no lumps remain, remove from the smoker and whisk until smooth. Keep warm.

Meanwhile, in a medium bowl, whisk the remaining 1 cup (250 mL) cream to medium peaks. Transfer to the fridge until ready to use.

In a medium stainless steel bowl set over a saucepan of simmering water, whisk the eggs, sugar, and coffee liqueur for 3 to 5 minutes, until the mixture forms soft peaks and has reached a thick ribbon stage— when you lift the whisk, the eggs should fall back into the bowl in ribbons that slowly merge back into the mixture. Gently fold the whipped eggs into the warm smoked chocolate mixture, then gently but thoroughly fold in the whipped cream. Transfer to the fridge until the mousse is set, at least 3 hours.

FLORENTINE COOKIES (MAKES ABOUT 20 THIN COOKIES)

½ cup (125 mL) unsalted butter

½ cup (125 mL) granulated sugar

2 tablespoons (30 mL) corn syrup

2 tablespoons (30 mL) heavy (35%) cream

¾ cup (175 mL) chopped black walnuts, more for garnish

SMOKED CHOCOLATE MOUSSE

8 ounces (225 g) chopped dark chocolate

2 cups (500 mL) heavy (35%) cream, divided

4 eggs

⅓ cup (75 mL) granulated sugar

2 ounces (60 mL) coffee liqueur (or any alcohol or liqueur you enjoy)

recipe and ingredients continues

Make the Meringue

In a medium bowl, whip the egg whites until frothy, about 2 minutes. (You can use an electric mixer.) Whisking constantly, slowly add the sugar a spoonful at a time and continue whipping to stiff, glossy peaks. Cover and refrigerate until ready to use. The meringue will last for 1 hour in the fridge.

Meanwhile, preheat the oven to 375°F (190°C). Line a baking sheet with parchment paper.

Bake the Florentine Cookies

Scoop 1 tablespoon (15 mL) of the dough and shape into a ball with your hands. Repeat, arranging the balls 2 inches (5 cm) apart on the prepared baking sheet. Bake until the cookies are paper thin and a dark caramel colour, 5 to 8 minutes. Transfer cookies to a rack and let cool completely. Store extra cookies in an airtight container on the counter for 1 day.

To Assemble

Spoon the meringue into bowls and torch with a kitchen torch for 5 to 10 seconds (or toast under the broiler for 2 to 3 minutes). Place a Florentine cookie on top, and then add a scoop of the smoked chocolate mousse on top of the cookie. Garnish with fresh berries and chopped black walnuts.

MERINGUE

4 egg whites
½ cup (125 mL) granulated sugar
Fresh berries, for garnish

Seeing deer eating green cedar leaves during the winter started me thinking about ways to cook with cedar. Cedar grows in abundance and is very easy to find and harvest, and I remembered learning in school that Indigenous people served cedar tea to the first settlers in Canada to cure their scurvy. Using this as inspiration, at Antler we started to incorporate cedar into our cocktails, and then I thought of creating a sweet tea and freezing it to make a cedar sorbet for dessert. The sorbet tastes incredibly refreshing—like the sweet smell of the forest.

CEDAR SORBET

Serves 4 to 6

In a medium saucepan, combine the water, cedar, and sugar. Stir to combine, bring to a simmer, and simmer for 10 minutes. Strain through a fine-mesh sieve into a medium bowl. Stir in the lemon zest and juice. Let cool to room temperature.

If using an ice-cream machine, cover and refrigerate the mixture until cold. Pour the mixture into the machine and churn according to the manufacturer's instructions until the sorbet has a smooth frozen consistency. Depending on your machine this could take up to 30 minutes. Scrape the sorbet into an airtight container and freeze until firm, 2 to 3 hours.

If you do not have an ice-cream machine, after the mixture has cooled to room temperature, place the bowl in the freezer for 30 minutes. Whisk the mixture, then return the bowl to the freezer. Continue to whisk every 30 minutes until the mixture is completely frozen and the ice is chunky, more like an iced granita. This can take several hours. At this point, cover and store the sorbet in the freezer until ready to serve.

Preheat the oven to 200°F (100°C).

Place a handful of cedar leaves on a baking sheet and toast until dry, 15 to 20 minutes. Try not to let the leaves brown. Mince the dried cedar leaves with a knife or, using a mortar and pestle or spice grinder, grind the leaves to a fine powder.

Divide the cedar sorbet among chilled small bowls. Garnish with a sprinkle of the minced or ground cedar leaves, and serve immediately.

2⅔ cups (650 mL) water
1 cup (250 mL) chopped green cedar boughs, more for garnish
⅔ cup (150 mL) granulated sugar
Zest and juice of 1 lemon

An Antler classic, this drink is almost like a cocktail sauce, because of the rich and spicy flavours of the tomato Caesar mix and grated fresh horseradish. Don't skip the prawn garnish.

SPOT PRAWN CAESAR

Serves 1

Make the Rimmer

In a small jar, with a lid, mix together all the ingredients. The rimmer mixture can be stored for up to 6 months.

Poach the Spot Prawns

In a medium pot, combine the water, white wine, vinegar, salt, peppercorns, and lemon juice. Bring to a boil.

Meanwhile, in a large bowl, combine 4 cups (1 L) of ice cubes and 4 cups (1 L) of water; set aside.

Once the pot is boiling, add the prawns. Remove from the heat and let the prawns poach for 1 to 3 minutes, until they are red and firm. Remove the prawns with a spider or slotted spoon and immediately put them in the ice bath. Once cool, drain the prawns and store in an airtight container in the fridge for up to 4 days.

Make the Cocktail

Evenly spread the rimmer mixture in a small plate wide enough to fit the rim of the glass you are using. Run the lemon wedge along the rim of the glass, then dip the rim into the rimmer mixture and twist slightly to make sure the rim is evenly coated.

Add the ice cubes to the glass. Add the vodka, mirin, Worcestershire sauce, Tabasco, Sriracha, horseradish, and Caesar mix. Stir until mixed well. Garnish with a poached prawn.

RIMMER (MAKES ENOUGH FOR 10 COCKTAILS)

2 tablespoons (30 mL) Spice Ash (page 73)

2 tablespoons (30 mL) celery salt

2 teaspoons (10 mL) black pepper

2 teaspoons (10 mL) red chili flakes

1 teaspoon (5 mL) cayenne pepper

POACHED SPOT PRAWNS (MAKES ENOUGH FOR 10 COCKTAILS)

8 cups (2 L) water

½ cup (125 mL) dry white wine

2 tablespoons (30 mL) white vinegar

1 tablespoon (15 mL) kosher salt

1 teaspoon (5 mL) black peppercorns

Juice of 1 lemon

10 spot prawns

COCKTAIL

1 lemon wedge

3 to 5 ice cubes

1½ ounces (45 mL) vodka

½ ounce (15 mL) mirin

2 dashes of Worcestershire sauce

2 dashes of Tabasco

2 drops of Sriracha sauce

1 teaspoon (5 mL) freshly grated horseradish

½ cup (125 mL) Caesar mix

1 poached spot prawn, for garnish

Sumac is the perfect addition to this classic Italian spritz because it adds lemon flavour without adding acidity to the drink and balances the sweetness of the Aperol. We forage a variety of ingredients from the forest to use in various cocktail infusions at Antler. It's a great way to add a fresh flavour sense from the woods to our cocktail creations. Using sumac is an easy way to do this at home.

SUMAC SPRITZ

Serves 1

Make the Sumac-Infused Aperol
Place the sumac berries in a 1-quart (1 L) mason jar. Pour in the Aperol, seal the jar, and let steep at room temperature for 4 days. Strain through a fine-mesh sieve and return the Aperol to the mason jar. The infused Aperol will keep indefinitely.

Make the Cocktail
Rim a wine glass with the ground sumac: pour the sumac powder onto a small plate, dip the rim of the glass in water, then dip it in the powder to coat the rim evenly.

Add the ice cubes to the glass. Pour in the infused Aperol. Add the Prosecco and soda water. The bubbles will do the mixing for you. Garnish with an orange peel.

SUMAC-INFUSED APEROL (MAKES ENOUGH FOR 10 COCKTAILS)
1 cup (250 mL) sumac berries
2 cups (500 mL) Aperol

COCKTAIL
1 tablespoon (15 mL) ground sumac
4 to 6 ice cubes
1½ ounces (45 mL) Sumac-Infused Aperol
2 ounces (60 mL) Prosecco
2 ounces (60 mL) soda water
1 orange peel, for garnish

Wild mint grows beside rivers, streams, and lakes starting in early spring and into late fall, making it a perfect herb to add to your drinks all summer long. I love it in this mojito, a classic cocktail that relies on fresh mint to achieve its refreshing taste.

WILD MINT MOJITO

Serves 1

Muddle 3 of the lime wedges with the mint in a Collins glass. Add the ice, rum, simple syrup, and soda water and stir well. Garnish with the remaining lime wedge.

4 lime wedges, divided
¼ cup (60 mL) wild mint leaves
¼ cup (60 mL) crushed ice
1½ ounces (45 mL) white rum
1½ ounces (45 mL) simple syrup
¼ cup (60 mL) soda water

Juniper is in the pine family and grows all over North America, Europe, and Asia. It is a primary flavouring in gin. By infusing store-bought gin with wild juniper, the clean notes of pine and hints of citrus really emerge. Juniper also has some homeopathic properties as an anti-inflammatory, diuretic, antiseptic, stomachic, antimicrobial, and antirheumatic. I'll drink to that.

WILD JUNIPER NEGRONI

Serves 1

Make the Juniper-Infused Gin
Place the juniper needles and berries in a 1-quart (1 L) mason jar. Pour in the gin, seal the jar, and let steep at room temperature for 4 days. Strain through a fine-mesh sieve and return the gin to the mason jar. The infused gin will keep indefinitely.

Prepare the Cocktail
In a large mixing glass, combine the juniper-infused gin, Campari, and sweet vermouth. Add the ice cubes. Stir for 15 seconds. Strain into a rocks glass over a large ice cube. Garnish with a sprig of juniper and orange peel.

WILD JUNIPER-INFUSED GIN (MAKES ENOUGH FOR 20 COCKTAILS)
1 cup (250 mL) juniper needles and berries
2 cups (500 mL) dry gin

COCKTAIL
¾ ounce (22 mL) Juniper-Infused Gin
¾ ounce (22 mL) Campari
¾ ounce (22 mL) sweet vermouth
3 ice cubes, for mixing
1 (2-inch/5 cm square) ice cube, for serving
1 sprig wild juniper, for garnish
1 orange peel, for garnish

When I was a kid, we used to pick wild blueberries at my family cottage in the summer. There are so many recipes I love making with them. You can use cultivated blueberries in this drink, or you can replace the berries with 1 tablespoon (15 mL) of Wild Blueberry Compote (page 219). Either way, this sour is a great addition to your summer cocktail repertoire.

Note that this cocktail is shaken twice, first without ice and a second time with ice. Shaking without ice is called a dry shake and helps the egg white turn into a thick foam.

WILD BLUEBERRY SOUR

Serves 1

Muddle the blueberries in a large mixing glass, then add the bourbon, simple syrup, and lemon juice and shake. Strain into a cocktail shaker. Add the egg white and shake for 30 seconds. Add the ice and shake for 30 seconds to 1 minute—you're looking to develop a nice thick egg white foam. Strain into a coupe glass. Garnish with the cherry bark vanilla bitters, and a mint leaf.

⅓ cup (75 mL) fresh wild blueberries

2 ounces (60 mL) bourbon

1 ounce (30 mL) simple syrup

1 ounce (30 mL) fresh lemon juice

1 ounce (30 mL) egg white (from 1 egg)

6 to 8 ice cubes

5 drops of cherry bark vanilla bitters

Fresh mint leaf, for garnish

This drink was one of the first wild-inspired cocktails we devised at Antler after I decided I wanted to incorporate our wild philosophy into the restaurant's cocktail list. Infusing the gin with cedar gives it woody and floral notes reminiscent of the forest. Cedar is probably the easiest and simplest ingredient to forage because it's so common in North America. If you don't have a cedar bush growing in your backyard, ask one of your neighbours if you can trim a few boughs from theirs.

CEDAR SOUR

Serves 1

Make the Cedar-Infused Gin

Preheat the oven to 300°F (150°C). Arrange the cedar boughs on a parchment-lined baking sheet and heat them in the oven for 5 minutes. Let cool to room temperature. Transfer the cedar to a 1-quart (1 L) mason jar and pour in the gin. Seal the jar and let steep at room temperature for 4 days. Strain through a fine-mesh sieve and return the gin to the mason jar. The infused gin will keep indefinitely.

Make the Cedar Powder

Preheat the oven to 200°F (100°C).

Arrange the chopped cedar boughs in a single layer on a parchment-lined baking sheet. Dehydrate for 15 to 20 minutes in the oven, making sure not to toast the cedar to a brown colour. The boughs should remain green but be easy to crumble. Use a spice grinder or food processor to pulverize the dehydrated cedar to a fine powder. Strain out any large chunks using a fine-mesh sieve. Store in an airtight container at room temperature for up to 1 month.

Prepare the Cocktail

In a cocktail shaker, combine the cedar-infused gin, lemon juice, egg white, and simple syrup. Dry-shake for 30 seconds. Add the ice and shake for 1 minute. Strain into a coupe glass and garnish with the aromatic bitters and a sprinkle of cedar powder.

CEDAR-INFUSED GIN (MAKES ENOUGH FOR 10 COCKTAILS)

½ pound (225 g) green cedar boughs, large brown woody stems removed (about 5 handfuls of cedar boughs)

3 cups (750 mL) dry gin

CEDAR POWDER

½ cup (125 mL) chopped green cedar boughs

COCKTAIL

2 ounces (60 mL) Cedar-Infused Gin

1 ounce (30 mL) fresh lemon juice

1 ounce (30 mL) egg white (from 1 egg)

1 ounce (30 mL) simple syrup

6 to 8 ice cubes

Aromatic bitters, for garnish

Cedar powder, for garnish

In western British Columbia the blackberry bushes grow to be 15 feet high—bigger than I have ever seen—and it feels like they stretch for miles. The locals call them B.C. barbed wire. You can forage pails and pails of them when they're in season, but you may need to fight off the bears. This cocktail was inspired one summer when I was picking them with my family on Vancouver Island. Make it with vodka or gin, depending on your taste.

WILD BLACKBERRY LEMONADE

Serves 1

Muddle the blackberries in a large mixing glass, then add the water, vodka or gin, lemon juice, and simple syrup. Stir for 5 seconds. Strain into an ice-filled Collins glass. Garnish with a lemon peel and fresh blackberries..

½ cup (125 mL) fresh wild
   blackberries, more for garnish
¼ cup (60 mL) water
1½ ounces (45 mL) vodka or gin
1 ounce (30 mL) fresh lemon
   juice
1 ounce (30 mL) simple syrup
4 to 6 ice cubes
Lemon peel, for garnish

This is our take on the classic Moscow mule. Wild ginger is not in the same family as the ginger you find in the grocery store, but it has a very similar flavour with additional floral notes and a spicy heat. Native to North America, it can easily be found in many forests across the continent during the spring and summer months. Wild ginger has an interconnected root system, so it is important not to pick more than 10 percent of a patch to ensure it will grow back.

WILD GINGER MULE

Serves 1

Make the Wild Ginger Syrup
In a small saucepan, combine the water, sugar, and wild ginger. Bring to a boil over medium-high heat and boil for 3 minutes. Let cool to room temperature. Strain the syrup into a mason jar with a lid and store in the fridge for up to 1 week.

Prepare the Cocktail
In a cocktail shaker, combine the vodka, wild ginger syrup, and lime juice. Add the ice cubes and shake for 15 seconds. Strain into a copper mule mug over crushed ice. Top with the ginger beer. Spear a piece of candied ginger with a cocktail pick and use it to garnish your drink along with a lime wheel and mint leaves.

WILD GINGER SYRUP (MAKES ENOUGH FOR 12 COCKTAILS)
1 cup (250 mL) water
1 cup (250 mL) granulated sugar
½ cup (125 mL) chopped wild ginger roots

COCKTAIL
1½ ounces (45 mL) vodka
1 ounce (30 mL) Wild Ginger Syrup
1 ounce (30 mL) fresh lime juice
6 to 8 ice cubes, for shaking
¼ cup (60 mL) crushed ice, for serving
½ cup (125 mL) ginger beer
Candied ginger, for garnish
Lime wheel, for garnish
Fresh mint leaves, for garnish

A timeless classic made Antler style with homemade maple syrup and maple fudge. We use maple as a sweetener in many of our desserts, and we like the way it adds a twist to the traditional subtle sweetness of this cocktail. You can make this cocktail with your favourite whisky or rye.

MAPLE OLD-FASHIONED

Serves 1

In a mixing glass, combine the whisky or rye, maple syrup, and aromatic bitters. Add the ice cubes and stir for 10 seconds. Strain into a rocks glass over a large ice cube. Garnish with maple fudge and an orange peel.

2 ounces (60 mL) whisky or rye
½ ounce (15 mL) pure maple
    syrup
3 drops of aromatic bitters
6 to 8 ice cubes, for mixing
1 (2-inch/5 cm square) ice cube,
    for serving
1 piece of Maple Fudge
    (page 243), for garnish
Orange peel, for garnish

Pawpaw is Canada's only tropical-tasting wild fruit, growing only in southern Ontario. In the United States it grows in many of the eastern states. It looks like a smaller version of a green mango that has blemish spots, and the fruit's flesh tastes like a mix of mango and banana with a smooth, custard-like texture. It is exciting to use this native fruit because it is quite rare to find, but the good news is people are starting to farm it. Look for it at your local farmers' market at the end of August and into September. This drink is refreshing with a tropical twist.

TROPIC PAWPAW

Serves 2

Cut the pawpaw in half lengthwise and remove the seeds, scoop out the flesh, and purée in a high-speed blender.

In a cocktail shaker, combine the pawpaw purée, vodka, and simple syrup. Add the ice cubes and shake for 15 seconds. Strain into coupe glasses and garnish each with a dried lemon wheel.

1 fresh pawpaw
3 ounces (90 mL) vodka
2 ounce (60 mL) simple syrup
6 to 8 ice cubes
Dried lemon wheels, for garnish

This cocktail is a showstopper. Torching a piece of applewood with a propane or butane torch and inverting the glass overtop will fill the room with a smoky aroma and provide a visual show for your guests too. This cocktail is a lot of fun to make, and the smoke from the applewood complements the smoky, peaty taste of the Scotch whisky so well. The cherry and chocolate bitters adds a touch of sweetness to cut the smoke.

APPLEWOOD SMOKE BARREL

Serves 1

Place the applewood chips on an old metal tray. Using a kitchen torch, light the chips for 10 to 20 seconds, until you can see red embers. You want to create smoke here, so be sure to carefully blow out any flames. Invert a rocks glass over the chips. Allow the smoke to fill the glass for at least 30 seconds.

While the smoke is filling the glass, in a mixing glass, combine the Scotch whisky, maple syrup, and chocolate bitters. Add the ice cubes and stir for 15 seconds. Revert the smoked rocks glass so the smoke bellows out, add a large ice cube, and strain the cocktail overtop. Garnish with a fresh or preserved cherry.

Small handful of applewood chips

2 ounces (60 mL) Scotch whisky

½ ounce (15 mL) pure maple syrup

3 drops of chocolate bitters

6 to 8 ice cubes, for mixing

1 (2-inch/5 cm square) ice cube, for serving

1 cherry (fresh or preserved, see page 137), for garnish

This one is for the meat lover. Venison jerky adds a meaty, salty flavour that blends nicely with the honey herbal flavour of the Drambuie in this smoky Scotch cocktail. I suggest using a peaty, smoky Scotch whisky for this cocktail.

RUSTY ANTLER

Serves 1

Make the Venison Jerky

In a medium saucepan, bring the ale to a boil. Reduce the heat and simmer until the ale is reduced to about ½ cup (125 mL). Add the soy sauce, Worcestershire sauce, maple syrup, peppercorns, chili flakes, and salt. Remove from the heat and let cool to room temperature.

Place the venison in an airtight container, cover with the ale mixture, and marinate in the fridge overnight. Discard the marinade. Pat dry and place in a dehydrator set to 150°F (65°C). (If you do not have a dehydrator, lay the meat strips on a baking sheet and place in a preheated 150°F/65°C oven.) Check the doneness of the meat after 4 hours. The jerky is ready when it is dry and leathery in texture. If it's not ready after 4 hours, check again every 30 minutes until the proper doneness is achieved. Store the jerky in an airtight container or sealed vacuum bag in the fridge for up to 1 month or in the freezer for up to 6 months.

Make the Jerky-Infused Drambuie

Combine 2 ounces (55 g) of the venison jerky and Drambuie in a 1-pint (500 mL) mason jar, seal the jar, and let steep in the fridge for 1 week before using. The infused Drambuie will keep in the fridge for 3 months.

Prepare the Cocktail

Add the Scotch whisky, jerky-infused Drambuie, and bitters to a mixing glass. Add the ice cubes and stir for 15 seconds. Strain into a rocks glass over a large ice cube. Garnish with a piece of venison jerky.

VENISON JERKY

2 cups (500 mL) ale or lager

1 cup (250 mL) light soy sauce

¼ cup (60 mL) Worcestershire sauce

2 tablespoons (30 mL) pure maple syrup

1 tablespoon (15 mL) black peppercorns

1 teaspoon (5 mL) red chili flakes

1 teaspoon (5 mL) kosher salt

1 pound (450 g) venison loin or muscle free of fat and sinew, sliced into ¼-inch (5 mm) thick strips

JERKY-INFUSED DRAMBUIE (MAKES ENOUGH FOR 30 COCKTAILS)

2 ounces (55 g) venison jerky

1½ cups (375 mL) Drambuie

COCKTAIL

1¾ ounces (50 mL) Scotch whisky

⅓ ounce (10 mL) Jerky-Infused Drambuie

3 drops of black walnut bitters

6 to 8 ice cubes, for mixing

1 (2-inch/5 cm square) ice cube, for serving

1 piece venison jerky, for garnish

Rosehips can be found in the late fall after the petals fall from the rose bushes, but they are best harvested after the first frost. Similar to the grapes that are used to make ice wine, rosehips develop a sweeter, jammier flavour when the temperature drops. You may have to fight the birds and squirrels for them, but you won't have to go far to find them if you have roses in your garden at home.

WAR OF ROSES

Serves 1

Make the Rose-Infused Bourbon

Place the rosehips in a 1-quart (1 L) mason jar. Add the bourbon, seal the jar, and let steep at room temperature for at least 4 days before using. Strain through a fine-mesh sieve and return the bourbon to the mason jar. The infused bourbon will keep indefinitely.

Make the Rosemary Syrup

Combine the sugar, water, and fresh rosemary in a small saucepan and bring to a boil. Let boil for about 4 minutes. Let cool to room temperature. Strain the syrup into an airtight container and store in the fridge for up to 1 week.

Prepare the Cocktail

In a cocktail shaker, combine the rose-infused bourbon, rose gin, rosemary syrup, lemon juice, and rosewater. Add the ice and shake for 15 seconds. Strain into a rocks glass over a large ice cube. Garnish with dried rose petals and rosemary.

ROSE-INFUSED BOURBON (MAKES ENOUGH FOR 15 COCKTAILS)

2 cups (500 mL) rosehips
2 cups (500 mL) bourbon

ROSEMARY SYRUP (MAKES ENOUGH FOR 10 TO 12 COCKTAILS)

1 cup (250 mL) granulated sugar
1 cup (250 mL) water
1 cup (250 mL) fresh rosemary leaves

COCKTAIL

1 ounce (30 mL) Rose-Infused Bourbon
1 ounce (30 mL) rose gin (can be purchased)
1 ounce (30 mL) Rosemary Syrup
1 ounce (30 mL) fresh lemon juice
⅓ ounce (10 mL) rosewater
6 to 8 ice cubes, for shaking
1 (2-inch/5 cm square) ice cube, for serving
Crushed dried rose petals and fresh rosemary, for garnish

ACKNOWLEDGMENTS

From Michael Hunter

I'd like to thank my mom for teaching me how to cook when I was a kid, taking me everywhere with you as a young boy and exposing me to all facets of life, ingraining in me that there is no such word as *can't* in life.

Ali, my wife, you are my rock, thank you for all of your love and support in following my dreams, and thank you for putting up with my never-ending hunting, foraging, and fishing trips. Thanks for letting me drag you and the kids through the mosquito-infested woods in my eternal search for mushrooms.

To my dad, thanks for your wisdom and guidance whenever I need it.

To all the chefs I have ever worked with, you inspired me and taught me everything you knew, always pushing me to be better.

To all of the staff at Antler, none of this would be possible without you. Thank you for believing in me. Your dedication to the restaurant and to our guests is incredible.

To Jody Shapiro, my honorary older brother, this has been an incredible journey.

To Joe Rogan, thank you for sharing your platform with me, giving me a larger voice, and for having my back when times were tough.

To Alex Atala for inspiring me to give back to the community and showing me the Brazilian culture, food, and wilderness.

Steve, Dave, and Frank with Organic Ocean, thank you for all the fishing adventures and education on sustainable fishing as well as sending us the best products possible.

Andrea Magyar and Penguin Random House Canada, thank you for believing in me and this book.

Daniel Haas and the entire Mossy Oak family, thank you for all your support.

Denis Seguin, for all your help with the essays.

Derick Dubblestyne, thank you for all your hard work at Antler and for helping with the cocktail recipes.

To the guests of Antler and readers of this book, thank you! I hope this book inspires you to pick something wild from the earth and eat it, and forever question where your food comes from.

From Jody Shapiro

Thank you to Denis Seguin and Leslie Anderson for suggestions and inspiration. Thank you to Aleksander Przulj, Howie Beck, Daniel Blaufuks, and David Wharnsby for endless advice and friendship. My mother, Vivian, and Rowland; and my father, Joel, and Miriam; and my brother Todd—this book would not have happened without family supporting us in all areas. Noriko for the gyoza, Alejandro for his love of cavatelli, and the largest thank you to my wife, Kaori, always standing strong and supportive beside me and encouraging me to pursue all my dreams. Credit is also due to the entire staff at Antler for understanding that a restaurant is more than getting good food on a plate; it is also about taking great care of our guests, and allowing Michael and me the time to explore the full potential of what we've all created. And, of course, my brother from another mother, the Hunter Chef. It's amazing how much one book has changed my life. From our first coffee, talking about food and photography, to six years, 11,000 photos, one restaurant, and twenty employees later, it's been an incredible journey with non-stop learning along the way. Thank you for the friendship and for everything you have taught me about food, cooking, and the incredible treasures found in the wilds of Canada.

INDEX